Matthew

Fishing

for Kids

A Complete Illustrated Guide to Fishing.

Basics, Tips and Techniques Easy explained.

Table of Contents

Introduction

Fishing is one of the best ways of relaxing and spending time with your kid, while he or she learns a thing or two. If done right, your kid will fall in love with the exercise so much that he will want to fish whenever a chance presents itself. Many people who enjoy the sport believe that, fishing entails more than just trapping fish. It has both an accomplishment and patience aspect: traits that are desirable not only in adults, but also in kids. If you have ever been interested in knowing what kids need to know about fishing to get started, then read on.

What should your kids know about fishing to get started?

Fishing is more of an adventure

Let your kid understand that you are going out to have fun and that they are not restricted to just fishing. Depending on how old he/she is, you should allow him or her to wade in the water, catch frogs, skip stones, play ball, float sticks and so on. Make it fun for your kid so that he will want to go "fishing" again in future. You can also let him bring friends, but not too many.

Go where there are plenty of easy to catch fish

Make your child understands that, if he wants to catch fish, he should go where the fish are. Bluegill and Sunfish are the best for young children. These fish are usually cooperative and easily reachable along the shoreline. They may be small, but that is not a problem. The most important thing is to catch fish.

It is okay to make mistakes

Be patient with your kid(s). Make sure that you have enough time to fish without distractions. It is okay if they make mistakes in the process of learning. If they do, laugh with them and keep encouraging them to learn as they have fun.

Explain to them the importance of being safe

Make your child understand that he or she should wear a life jacket whether he or she is on the boat, shore, or dock. You should also avoid steep banks. It is advisable to use barbless hooks instead of the ordinary hooks – this keeps the incidences of having hooks stuck in the tender skin to a minimum.

You can also practice casting with your child in the backyard before going fishing. You can use Practice Casting plugs since they do not have hooks and work perfectly in the backyard. Practice makes a big difference when it comes to baiting the fish.

Teach them how to use fishing equipment

Make sure that the rod and reel fit your child's hands. Shorter rods – 4 to 5 feet long – with smaller reels are much more comfortable. An adult-sized rod and reel can frustrate your child because it may be too difficult to use. You should also use bobbers since they are not only fun to watch, they also show if you are getting a bite. A little tackle box is also a good way to encourage your child to keep his or her fishing gear in an organized manner.

Encourage them to use live bait

Earthworms are the ideal baits for a first-timer. They are not only easy to hook, but also ideal for catching fish in lakes, ponds and streams. You can buy them in bait shops or simply dig them up in your garden. Mealworms and minnows are the best. Artificial baits are more effective if used after gaining some fishing experience.

Help your child cast

Upon reaching the local lake, look for the area that has ample room to cast and a bank that has a gentle slope. You can find Sunfish along the shorelines. After baiting the hook, rest the bobber on the line on top of the hook. This varies depending on the water depth; however, a depth of 18 to 24 inches is just fine. Help your kid(s) cast and then take time to observe the bobber. Let it rest for some time, then reel it a little further and, again, let it rest for some time.

If you catch fish, you have two choices; you can store it in your ice chest and fry it afterwards, kids love the taste of a freshly caught fish; or release the catch. You should minimize the time the fish is out of the water if your intention is to release it. Also, exercise caution while removing the hook. Let your child admire the fish the entire time. Knowledge of your area's fishing regulations is also important.

Make it a short exercise

Do not expect your child to enjoy fishing for more than two hours if it is his or her first time. An hour or two is enough fishing time. Afterwards, you can enjoy an outdoor activity together, for example, a picnic or play ball. It is important to remember that spending time enjoying the outdoors is your main objective.

The Take Away

Fishing is a fun, outdoor activity. Safely introducing your kid(s) to the sport is an important part of both your lives: you will both reminisce the good times you had outdoors together. The above guide is a manual on what kids need to know about fishing to get started; you can always refer to it whenever you want to take your kid(s) fishing.

Basics of Fishing

Dropping a line in the water might seem pretty simple. To do this, you need a fishing rod, reel, bait, and some lures. If you are using bait, then you need to tie a simple rig of a little hook to a small sinker that helps to drop the bait into the water where the fish can bite.

A Uni Knot

If you don't know how to tie a basic knot, then you need to learn to tie fishing knots to attach the rigs and tie the hooks. The more you practice, the easier it becomes. In this section, you will learn about tying a simple uni knot that you can teach the kids when you take them fishing.

The uni knot is one of the most basic fishing knots and it is easy to learn. It is quite strong as well. Do you know how to tie shoelaces? If yes, then this is a very simple knot to master. There are four simple steps that you need to follow.

The first step is to take the hook and run a line through the eye of the hook and then double back to create a loop by letting the tag end over the double fishing line.

Now, you must wrap the tag end around the double line by going through the loop you created in the previous step.

You need to repeat this process six times to strengthen the knot.

Once you do this, you need to moisten the line and then pull the main line to tighten the knot.

If you aren't aware of what the tag end is, then it is the end of the line. You must always moisten the line to prevent any friction; it also prevents the knot from sliding along the line. You can wet the line by putting the knot in your mouth. You must also cut away any extra tagline that's there but never cut it too close to the knot. If you cut it too close to the knot, the knot will slide away.

Running Sinker Rig

You can use a running sinker rig to catch a wide array of fish in estuaries and even deep water. It is quite reliable and simple to make.

You need about a meter of the trace line or you can even use the main line if you don't have any trace line. Now, ask the child to tie a hook on one end and a swivel on the other end with the help of a uni knot.

Now, the child needs to thread a ball sinker through the main line and use a uni knot to join it to the other end of the swivel.

Set up Rod and Reel

You need to teach the child to set up the rod and the reel if you want to teach the child to fish. To set up the rod, the child needs to thread the line from the reel through the eyelets present on the rod and then pull it through so that a swivel, hook, or a clip can be attached to the end of the line. The hook and the sinker arrangement or anything else that you place at the end of the line is known as a rig. There are various types of rigs available and the one that you select will depend on the type of fish you want to catch and where you are fishing. You will need a small hook and sinker if you are taking your children fishing in calm water, whereas a big sinker and hook are essential if you are beach fishing.

Attach Bait

There are different types of baits you can use like squids, prawns, bread, and even worms. According to the species of fish you want to catch, the bait you use will differ. The size of the bait you use needs to be proportional to the hook you attach to the rod. If you want to catch small fish, then you need small pieces of bait and for a bigger species of fish, you need a larger hook or bait. While you are attaching bait to the hook, always ask the child to keep a portion of the barbed section of the hook exposed to increase the chances of catching fish.

Attach Lure

Lures are quite easy to store, and you can keep them in your tackle box. These come in handy especially when the fish are feeding close to the surface. Use lures when you notice fish close to the surface of the water. To attach a lure, ask the child to tie a small clip to the end of the trace line. Then the child merely needs to attach the lure to the clip. You can unclip the lure later if the fish don't bite.

The Benefits of Fishing for Children

Fishing is truly recognized as one of the, if not the, most relaxing sport known to man today. Offering serene and peaceful surroundings of quiet bodies of water or majestic ocean locations, fishing presents the fisherman with hours of relaxation and quiet. The skills required for fishing are minimal, and can indeed be easily taught to children. Learning the simple techniques of applying bait to a fishing line, and mastering the simple art of casting your fishing reel, are pretty much the only learned skills you need. Many people use their fishing time to get lost in the quiet of the world around them, to embrace the stillness and the calm that the beautiful waters have to offer, and to enjoy the thrill of the "chase" as they attempt to lure in and catch that trophy fish of theirs.

Benefits of Fishing

Obviously, the benefits of fishing are many. As we have mentioned above the peacefulness, the serenity, the excitement of catching that elusive fish, in addition to the exercise of body and mind that it offers, are some of the most obvious benefits of fishing. For many, fishing and actually catching fish, is a good food source as well, and even a moral boost that one needs to feel better about themselves or perhaps to feel accomplished. Living in such a fast-paced world so filled with drama and abundant challenges, many find fishing to be the solution to all the ongoing tasks and responsibilities. After a long week of gruesome work, whether in an office environment or plant/warehouse environment, fishing seems like such a perfect calm after the storm. Long hours of work, endless problem solving tasks, countless deadlines, and timelines to be met, can surely make the average person feel a bit overwhelmed and flat out exhausted. So is it any wonder that casting a fishing reel into a majestic, beautiful body of water, with nothing but sunshine, blue skies, and quiet surrounding you, is looked upon as a safe haven away from all the hustle and bustle?

Children and Fishing

Children are every bit as overwhelmed and exhausted as adults specifically with their school demands, homework assignments, home chores, and young commitments. Many times children become so overwhelmed that they feel as though there is no way to overcome the stress and find simple happiness in their every day. Teaching children to fish can most assuredly help them to find peace and solace away from all their young hustle and bustle. Fishing will not only offer them a means of quiet and serenity, but will also teach children about techniques and, even more importantly, teach them patience. We all know how patient you have to be when fishing and indeed, nowadays, many a child needs to learn patience along with responsibility. What a splendid and exciting way to teach the art of patience to children than through a handful of pleasant fishing adventures together.

Parents can enlighten their children on the beauty of nature as well, and help educate them on the many simple things that surround them every day that many times go unnoticed. Getting children interested and involved in the sport of fishing need not be a difficult challenge. Again, reminding the children of the fast pace they live every day, and the demands that are constantly made on their young lives, should entice them to want to engage in some activities that can take away all that hurry, and the drama that school, home chores, homework, and even peer pressure can present. Certainly many children look to their television, video games, computers, and cell phones as a means of escape, but these avenues are not beneficial to their bodies and minds. Explaining to them that there is not only comfort and peace in the very soothing sport of fishing, but also opportunities for competing in age restricted fishing tournaments, can lead children to find a devoted interest in the sport and in the fun-filled competitions offered.

There are many summer events that involve fishing activities, whether town events or summer camps, that can definitely hold the attention and interest of children if they are so guided. Assuring them that they are capable of learning this skillful but simple sport, and can find many hours of fun and relaxation engaging in it, is a sure fire way of capturing the attention of your young ones.

Conclusion

Once you have been able to instruct your children on the easy to learn techniques of fishing, the rewards will be many for all. Spending quality time together with your children fishing is not only beneficial to the child, but by all means a benefit to mom and dad as well since there seems to be so little quality family time together available these days. Teaching your children to fish will also take the attention away from the endless list of technology related activities that offer little to true benefit to children. Fishing is by every means a healthy sport and exercise that is sure to capture and hold tight the attention and interest of children if only mom and dad take the necessary time to teach the sport and all its many benefits to them.

Teach Fishing in Ten Steps

Whenever you decide to teach a kid to fish, you need to keep a couple of things in mind. You need to ensure that the child is safe and that they experience their fishing experience in a stress-free environment. Follow the simple steps explained in this chapter to teach kids to fish. Once you check the last item off this list, you will know that you are ready to have some fun on the water and maybe even catch dinner!

Step 1: Find the Right Location

Remember, the primary objective of any fishing trip is to catch fish! Duh! So, if you want to avoid sad faces or a broken heart because you weren't able to catch any fish, then you need to make sure that you catch some fish. You need to find the right location. This is an essential step regardless of whether you want to sail on a boat or a kayak, or you plan to stay ashore or fish from a dock or not.

If you have a local fishing club, then you can ask them for advice. If not, you can always ask for advice at the local tackle shop. Also, you can ask for other information like suggestions for the best baits for a specific location, the kind of license you will need, and any other questions related to fishing regulations. If possible, then take the child along, as the child will also learn about the different aspects of this activity apart from catching fish.

Step 2: Organization is Essential

Once you start to prep for the fishing trip, you need to make a checklist. It will reduce the possibility of any last-minute stress and you will not have to worry about forgetting anything. So, check your list twice, when you pack your stuff and once before you head out. Here is a sample of a checklist that you can use before you head out on a fishing trip.

Like any outdoor activity, fishing requires specific gear like a fishing rod, tackle boxes, bait, hooks, lures, nets, and reels.

Snacks: you must never forget to carry snacks with you since you will be spending a lot of time on the open water. It is always a good idea to have a couple of snacks handy. You never know when the little ones might be hungry!

Drinks: carrying drinking water is quintessential to any fishing trip and you must not leave the house without a couple of bottles of drinking water at least. Being surrounded by water but being unable to consume it can be quite stressful. When you are out in the open for a long time, the elements of nature like the sun can cause dehydration. So, it is always a good idea to carry a couple of bottles of water. Apart from this, you can pretty much stock up on anything that you want to drink.

Sunscreen: fishing is an outdoor activity and you will spend a lot of time exposed to the sun. Even if it is not hot outside, spending a lot of time under the sun can cause sunburn. You must not only carry sunscreen with you, but you must also not forget to use it. Overexposure to the sun can cause troubles for not just adults, but children as well.

Bug repellant: if you are fishing in a pond, lake or a river, it means that there will be plenty of flies and other insects around you that can distract you. Bugs can also make your trip quite unpleasant. You can purchase bug repellant from a local tackle shop and hit the water only after you buy bug repellant. You will certainly be thankful for it later.

Rain jackets: getting caught in the rain is quite common. If you have been fishing for a while, then you might have experienced a sudden downpour at some point in time or other. You need to remember that no one can predict the weather accurately and you never know when it changes, so instead of risking the rain, it is better to carry a raincoat with you.

Hat: just like sunscreen, the hat will also protect your head from the sun rays. It also makes it easy to observe surroundings without the glare of the sun hitting your eyes.

Sunglasses: when the sun is shining high overhead, it can be difficult to see beneath the surface of the water due to the color difference. Sunglasses offer some shade and you will be able to see what is going on below the surface. Apart from this, sunglasses offer protection from the glaring sun rays and any potential damage to your eyes.

First-aid kit: regardless of how careful you are, accidents cannot be prevented. You must always carry a first-aid kit with you.

Ensure that you carry all these necessary items with you whenever you decide to go fishing. You are not only responsible for your safety, but you are responsible for the safety of the child present with you.

Step 3: Safety First!

If you don't pay attention to various aspects of safety when you have children around water, then it can prove to be quite a disaster. The first and foremost thing that you must always take is a life jacket. In case someone falls into the water, the life jacket will keep them afloat. Hooks are essential for fishing, but they can be quite problematic if you don't handle them properly. Hooks have barbs, so you need to be extra careful when you let children anywhere near sharp objects. You can always use something to hide the hook within the bobber so that it is safe for casting, especially for kids.

Step 4: Discuss and Plan

Children tend to be naturally curious regardless of their sex, age, geographic location and such. So, it is a good idea to explain certain things to them before you go fishing together. You need to show them how to set up the hook and all other aspects of fishing. It might take the child a while to understand all this, so make sure that you are patient with them.

Step 5: Hold the Rod

The first thing you must teach your child is to hold the rod properly. Remember to teach the child to always keep the rod in front of themselves, in a 9-11 o'clock position. Pay close attention to the way the child grips the rod. Carefully explain the way the reel handle works and the way to react when the fish bites. You must always be patient with children and don't be harsh. After all, you need to remember that they came on the fishing trip to learn.

Step 6: Casting Technique

There are two casting techniques; these techniques are the overhead cast and the sidearm cast. Usually, professionals and experienced fishermen tend to use the former and the latter is better suited for beginners.

Before you teach kids how to perform the sidearm cast, you need to make sure that no one is in the way. Take a look around to see if the coast is clear and then cast away! Now, you need to bring back the rod and make sure it stays above your waist while you are doing so.

It might take a child a couple of tries before he or she can do it well. In fact, it is quite likely that the first couple of attempts will not be a success. This is the time for you to maintain your calm and let the child practice some more. The more a child tries, the better the child will get at casting, so keep encouraging the child. You must never forget that you are dealing with a child and never lose your calm.

Step 7: Gear

I've already mentioned that you will need fishing gear. Up until now, you were learning about the steps to follow while teaching a child to fish. This information will not do you much good if you don't have the right gear for your fishing trip. You will need the right bobber, bait and a lightweight fishing rod. You also need some spin cast somewhere between 3'6" and 5' for successfully fishing. You will learn more about this in the coming chapters.

Step 8: Live or Artificial Bait?

To start with, it is always a good idea to start with artificial bait. It might scare the children if they need to use worms or minnows on their first fishing trip. Not only are artificial baits attractive and durable, they are easy to use as well. You merely need to rig them on a 1/32 to 1/8-ounce jig and it will do the trick for you. The best option for kids is bait is a jig dangled under a tiny float with an occasional twitch. It will show the kid how the bait behaves in water and you can show them how to reel and retrieve.

Step 9: Land a Fish

Catching fish certainly requires a lot of patience. You need to teach your young students to hold the rod steadily. You also need to show them to slowly reel the bait in when the fish reaches the surface. Also, you must show the child how this is to be done and don't do everything by yourself. If the child wants to try and land the fish by himself or herself, then you must let them. You can help them by giving the necessary instructions on how they need to react. Also, maintain a casual environment so that the child doesn't hesitate while asking for help. When the process is complete, and your child lands a fish, you can either release it or keep it for dinner! If you want to release the fish, then ask the child to not simply drop it or throw it back into the water. Instead, you need to show the child to slowly put it back and release it when the fish is completely submerged in water. If you want to use the fish for dinner, then you need to explain harvesting and why some fish need to be returned to the water.

Step 10: Have Fun

One thing you must not forget is that this is a fun activity, so you need to have fun and make sure that the children have fun as well. If you want the kids to come back with you on other fishing trips, the trip needs to be enjoyable and memorable. Don't worry about the numbers and instead concentrate on having fun. You might or might not catch anything, but the memories you make during this process matter the most. The biggest catch you can make is to get the child interested in fishing. Also, don't forget to bring a camera along with you to capture all the fun you had.

Follow the simple steps discussed in this chapter to teach your child how to fish and get started with fishing. The way you introduce fishing will make all the difference. So, make the activity fun and engaging and the child will certainly want more of it.

Is Fishing a Good Activity for Kids?

When kids are not in school, or engaged in family activities, the majority of this younger population spends their time playing video games, or spends endless hours on their computers, iPads, and cell phones. It seems this world we live in does not encourage, nor enforce kids to participate in more outdoor activities that are, by far, much healthier and even more exciting for them. With the fast-paced world, we all live in, it seems many times that it is much easier for parents to simply allow their kids to amuse themselves, and partake in the advanced technology activities that are popular today.

However, it is critical to realize that physical activity, and indeed outdoor natural activities, are very important to the development, both physical and mental, of children of all ages. Spending endless hours utilizing technology can, in many cases, advance the mind, but does not in any way, whatsoever, offer physical development to children. There are an array of healthy and fun outdoor activities that will help kids of all ages, and fishing, by far, is one of them.

Teaching Kids Fishing

The actual sport of fishing is quite simple, and very easy to learn. Leaning the art of placing the bait on your line, and the skillful art of casting your rod, as well as proper technique for reeling in a fish, are the primary elements of fishing. Children of all ages can be taught these simple techniques, and are quite capable of mastering them as well. Teaching kids to fish, has a few very obvious benefits that are not only rewarding, but every bit as refreshing as well.

One of the most important benefits of fishing is the patience that is learned when engaging in this sport. Fishermen of all ages and genders, ultimately learn the value of patience as they experience their fishing adventures. For starters, it takes a lot of patience to be able to bait the rod, but most assuredly, the greatest patience comes into play after casting your rod, and setting in the stillness around you as you wait for the fish to bite. How truly patient you have to be, and what a spectacular character trait to teach all of our kids. In addition, when children learn to fish, they learn to appreciate the beauty of the nature that surrounds them, from the majestic waters, to the beautiful skies and greenery that are present. Fishing is indeed a very serene and passive sport offering much peace and tranquility to those who engage. Certainly kids nowadays could use more relaxing, and passive activities to engage in, rather than those loud video games and nonstop ringing cell phones.

Fishing affords children the luxury of embracing some of the finest nature in this world and when they actually make a catch, are overwhelmed by their own feelings of accomplishment. Like any sport, fishing offers its participants the element of competition, and when competing, and especially when you are a victor, the feelings of accomplishment are ever so rewarding to the child. As a result, children develop knowledge and skills from the exciting sport of fishing, knowledge and skills they can then turnaround and share with other kids.

Statistics have proven that children who engage in outdoor activities, including fishing, experience educational gains in social studies, science, and even the arts. Additionally, engaging in outdoor healthy activities increases the self-esteem of children, their problem solving abilities, all while increasing their motivation to learn new things. Further studies have proven that engaging in outdoor activities such as fishing, reduce negative stress in kids, and also can reduce symptoms of attention deficit disorder.

Overall teaching kids to fish reaps only positive rewards, and results in the lives of children of all ages. If you are in search of healthy, beneficial learning techniques for your children, then indeed start by teaching them to fish, and enjoy the newfound presence of their patience, self-esteem, motivation, sense of self-accomplishment, and ability to handle unsuspecting stress in their lives. Encouraging children to participate in all outdoor natural activities, including biking, swimming, and fishing, in place of video games and computers, is a spectacular parenting technique that is sure to present with happier, healthier, and more confident children; and isn't that exactly what all of us parents want for our precious children!

Useful Resources for the New Fisherman/Angler

Fishing is by far one of the most relaxing and popular of all outdoor sports today. Offering relaxation and comfort, while affording its participants the opportunity to find themselves immersed in some of the most refreshing and natural surroundings Mother Nature has to offer, fishing is truly one sport favored by people of all ages. In a world where lessons taught, and lessons learned are many, fishing offers its participants life lessons in patience, appreciation, acceptance, and the skills of fishing, all of which serve one well in life.

Though a great deal of fishing can be learned through doing, and developed over time, there is much about the sport that requires dedication and skill. For the new fisherman these techniques, along with the many how to tips can be learned and acquired by way of useful fishing resources. There are truly abundant fishing resources available today to assist the new fisherman. Some of the more popular resources are listed here below.

Resources for the New Fisherman

1. The Future Fisherman Foundation - This highly recognized fishing organization offers top of the line information and tools for all fishermen, including the new entry-level fisherman. Offering books, guides, handbooks, and programs that teach and acquaint individuals with all the rules and regulations of the sport, as well as state of the art activities and events, you are sure to find all that you need to know about fishing through this spectacular organization. With a simple mission statement focused on introducing youth to the sport of fishing, and a motto of "Ensuring the Future of Fishing", this popular resource, and its many accomplishments have contributed greatly to the health and well-being of our youth.

Programs that reach out to children of all ages to acquaint them with the sport of fishing, and the outdoors in general, offer much to the new fisherman as he sets his sights on learning this truly popular sport, and engaging in all the pleasures that fishing has to offer. The Future Fisherman Foundation is a highly reputable organization with a history of awards and outstanding accomplishments. Truly a foundation that has inspired many a youth, and offered all that is needed for those who share an interest in fishing, and the great outdoors, this amazing resource is a must use for all new, up and coming fishermen.

2. In-Fishermen (Magazine and television program) - This exciting and highly popular magazine and television program offers all the insight needed for the new fisherman. From fishing gear, places to fish, and types of fish, to fishing tools, reeling techniques, and specialized events, this state of the art magazine and television program offers much to the new fisherman looking to develop his fishing skills, and enhance his abilities over time. Offering informative articles and stories on the how to of fishing, the beginner fisherman is sure to find all that he is in search of through this handy resource. Gaining recognition in the sporting industry, as one of the most top of the line resources for fishing, In-Fishermen is a name familiar to anglers of all ages, and a resource that is sure to provide both know how and confidence to the excited beginner.

3. The Fisherman Magazine - This spectacular fishing resource is the largest fishing publication in all of the United States. Catering to anglers of all levels, including the new fisherman, this innovative and very informative magazine has all that the angler in you needs to know and learn. Recognized for offering the best all round fishing information available to man today, the Fisherman Magazine is a true "go to" resource for every fishermen, and yes, the new fisherman as well. Instructing its readers on fishing rules and regulations, fishing knots and rigs, a collection of published books, and an event calendar of fishing events in your area, the new angler is sure to find answers to all

his questions and concerns through this exciting and highly awarded magazine.

Fishing Poles and Lures

Teaching a child to fish is a fun activity. Keep in mind that you are teaching a child to fish, so using a large or a heavy fishing pole will defeat the purpose. Children don't care if they are going to catch a five-pound bass or three-inch bluegill. Children merely want to catch lots of fish. The idea is to bring them to a place where the fish will bite easily. This section will learn about the different fishing poles and lures you can use to teach fishing.

Hook and Worms

You can use Eagle Claw Snap-on plastic bobber floats that are available in many sizes. These are great when you are teaching children to fish with small poles. The bobber is slightly heavy, makes it easier to cast, and allows you to cast the shore's bait. A large bobber also gives the child a clear view of when the fish bite and the added weight keeps it submerged in water.

You can use an Eagle Claw Bait holder circle hook for a fishing pole. These hooks go perfectly well with bobbers. The barbs on this bait holder make it easier for the bait to hold on even when the fish start tugging on it. The circle hook needs to get caught in the fish's mouth. If you use J-hooks, make sure that you have no intention of releasing the fish back into the water.

A J-hook is hard to remove because it gets hooked quite deep in a fish's stomach and can injure the fish severely.

You can use a treble hook since they also work well with bobbers. These are the hooks that are used when fishing for trout. The three hooks present on the treble hook make it likely that at least one hook will catch the corner of a fish's mouth, and the fish doesn't swallow it. It is also quite helpful when you want to hide small amounts of bait in the hook. If you want a treble hook, please consider the Gama katsu Treble Hook- sizes 14 to 18.

Best Fishing Poles for Kids

You not only need to use the right bait and lure but having the right size of pole also makes it easier for the kids to fish.

The Shakespeare youth fishing pole has a reel with a push-button for toddlers. It is about two feet and six inches long and comes with a plastic practicing plug. This is suitable for children above the age of 4. It also comes in a different cartoon print. If your child is less than 5-years old, then you need to buy this fishing pole! You need to make sure that the child is holding on tightly to this pole. Since they are quite light, they can be tugged into the water when a big fish decides to bite.

Starter Rod and Reel Combo

Whenever you are selecting a fishing rod, you need to select one that is lightweight and is easy to use. It is always good to opt for a whirling pre-spooled rod and reel combo. The mechanism needs to be easy to use and simple to understand. Your little angler must be able to understand the basics of fishing without getting overwhelmed, or worse yet, frustrated!

The Kid Casters Youth Fishing Kits are a great option to start with. It comes with a 29.5-inch long fiberglass rod that is easy to use. The reel is also spooled with a 6-pound monofilament line, which is perfect for freshwater fishing. Remember, you need to keep your child's physical strength in mind when you select a fishing rod. After all, it is the child who needs to hold the rod and not you. Ideally, take the child along with you to the local tackle shop to select a reel and rod combo that works well for him or her. This fishing pole costs about $24 online.

Kid's Tackle Box

Every person interested in fishing needs a tackle box. When you are selecting a tackle box for a kid, you need something that is lightweight and secure. It also needs to include a couple of beginner's tools and must provide sufficient space to include jigs, spinners, crank baits, spoons, and plugs. The tackle box will essentially contain everything that a child will need to go fishing excluding the pole.

The Take Me Fishing tackle box is a good idea. It consists of a single tray box that is stocked with the bare essentials like hooks, sinkers, soft-body jigs, and bobbers. Also, the company that makes these tackle boxes donates a small portion of their proceeds to the Future Fisherman Foundation. You can buy this tackle box for $17.

Bobbers

When you are looking at bobbers, always opt for the Snap-On bobbers. These are easy to attach, and the kids don't need to tie them onto the line. Since you are just getting the children familiarized with fishing, it is always a good idea to start slow. Also, you are shopping for a child, so make sure that you select a bobber that is bright and colorful. A fisherman needs to spend a major chunk of their time watching the bobbers, so you might as well make sure that the child has something good to look at. Also, a bobber gives the first indication when a fish tugs on the bait and it is quite engaging when the bobber has fun designs on it.

The TMNT rattle bobbers are easy to snap on and look like the ninja turtles.

Soft Plastics

These are great when you are introducing the child to lure fishing. They look quite natural and their wiggly nature helps attract fish. You need soft plastic with a single hook on the jig head. This is easier to handle than bait with trebles. You can change the lures you use according to the level of comfort of the child.

Landing Net

You need a landing net that is rubber coated so it doesn't harm the scales of a fish and also reduces the chances of the fish getting stuck to the hook or getting tangled in the net. The Mad Bite's Foldable and Retractable Landing Nets are quite nice, so please do check them out before you buy a landing net. These nets have a hoop that's made of white e-glass that won't get dinged, unlike aluminum.

Fishing Pliers

You will need a pair of fishing pliers not just to secure the hooks and cut lines but also to unhook catches. You need fishing pliers regardless of whether you are going bone fishing in the Bahamas or fishing for crappie in Wisconsin. You need a pair of pliers that the child can hold onto easily, and the jaws of the pliers need to be suitable for usage in fresh as well as seawater. The Bass Pro Shop's XPS Aluminum Pliers are worth buying.

Fishing Gloves

You need to buy your child a pair of fishing gloves before you take them fishing. Look for a three-fingerless glove that frees up the thumb, middle finger and forefinger. These three fingers need to be unrestricted to improve the dexterity of the child casting the line.

Another item that you need to purchase is a life jacket or any other PFD. Find something that fits the child well and isn't too big or too small for the child.

Before you can take the children on a fishing trip, you need to make sure that they have all the necessary fishing equipment. You cannot teach anyone to fish without the necessary tools and the gear.

Live Bait

Using the natural food that fish eat is often the best way to catch them. Live bait often works when nothing else does, but getting the bait and keeping it alive can be a problem. Learn some live-bait basics and you should catch more and bigger fish.

Kinds of Live Bait

Some fish will eat just about anything that wiggles while others are very specific in their feeding habits. Although you can usually buy most kinds of live bait, catching it yourself is cheaper and guarantees fresh bait.

Sometimes getting the bait is almost as much fun as catching the fish, especially if you approach it that way.

Earthworms

Live earthworms are a basic bait for almost all kinds of freshwater fish and even some saltwater species. From a single red wiggler on a hook for bluegill to a gob of them on a hook for mullet, earthworms are an excellent bait. And you can find them in a lot of different kinds, from the small red wigglers to giant night crawlers. Some fish prefer one over the other but almost all fish will hit some kind of earthworm.

Using the kind of earthworm found near the waters you fish is usually best because they're used to eating them. Rains wash worms into the water so fish there see them often. But at times a different kind of bait can be good. Try big night crawlers even if they don't grow near where you fish. This change can make reluctant fish bite.

Freshwater and Saltwater Baitfish

Baitfish usually travel in schools and game fish will attack them and gorge on them. The most common kinds of baitfish in fresh water are shad and herring. Threadfin shad grow to a few inches long and are a warm-water species. Everything from crappie to catfish will eat them. Gizzard shad get much bigger, can tolerate much colder water, and are good bait for bigger fish.

Blueback herring are a saltwater species that has been trapped in some freshwater lakes during their spawning run and prospered there. Skipjack herring are bigger and have also been trapped in some freshwater lakes. Both are excellent bait for bigger game fish like striped bass and big largemouth bass. Alewives, another kind of small herring, are a popular bait, especially around the Great Lakes

Fishermen have introduced into the environment many kinds of exotic species by using them as bait. Never dump unused baitfish into the water at the end of the trip. They may start reproducing and that almost always creates problems for the native fish.

A large number of different kinds of saltwater baitfish make good bait. Menhaden, also called bunker or pogies, in the six-inch range are excellent for almost all kinds of bigger saltwater fish. Blue runner are a type of big open-water baitfish that are used for big-game fish like marlin. All kinds of herring are good in salt water, and mullet make good bait where they can be found. Ballyhoo, needlefish, pinfish, cigar minnows, and others are also good bait in salt water.

Crickets

Crickets and their cousin grasshoppers make good bait for pan fish in fresh water. Store-bought crickets are usually brown, which for some reason fish seem to prefer over wild black crickets. Drop a cricket into a bluegill bed and it usually won't have time to settle down before a fish eats it. Crickets can also be used to catch catfish and other species but they're best for bream.

Other Live Bait

Just about any kind of small critter can be used as live bait. Some common ones used in fresh water include:

• Catalpa worms

• Crayfish

• Frogs

• Grub worms

- Hellgrammites

- Leeches

- Mealworms

- Salamanders

- Wasp larvae

- Wax worms

And some popular saltwater baits include:

- Bloodworms

- Clams

- Crabs

- Eels

- Sandworms

- Shrimp

- Squid

Many saltwater baits also work well in fresh water for a variety of fish. Although most won't stay alive in fresh water, they can be fished dead or as cut bait for catfish and other bottom feeders. Eels will live in fresh water and are good bait for stripers, bass, and catfish. The same goes for the baits used mainly in freshwater fishing. They can be used live in salt water if they survive, but can also be used as cut bait or dead bait if they don't.

When to Use Each

Use live bait any time you want to catch fish! Depending on availability and your ability to keep bait alive, it will almost always out-fish any other kinds of baits. There may be some presentations that prohibit the use of live bait, but you can almost always find a way to present live bait to fish. Sometimes it may be slower to fish with live bait than with artificials but slowing down and using live bait will usually pay off in higher numbers of fish caught, as well as bigger fish landed.

Using live bait can create problems. Fish are usually hooked deeper and are harder to release alive when caught on live bait. Live bait like crawfish or minnows may also escape into waters where they are not native and establish populations that cause problems

Some waters may be fished with artificial bait, only. Check regulations before fishing with live bait to make sure it's legal. Be especially careful on trout steams, because many of them are artificial bait, only.

Live Bait for Fresh Water

Some freshwater fish such as walleye are known to be finicky eaters, so you almost always have to use live bait. A jig may not catch many walleye but tip it with a worm, leech, or minnow and they will bite. Both Bream and Crappie will hit small jigs and flies but prefer live worms and minnows most of the time.

For trophy bass a big live minnow like a golden shiner is hard to beat. Some guides in Florida specialize in shiner fishing because it produces lunker bass better than anything else. Almost as many big bass are caught on live crayfish, good bait for smallmouth and largemouth. Drop a crayfish down around a rock reef in the Great Lakes and you can land a trophy smallmouth.

Stripers and hybrids will hit live herring and shiners much better than they'll hit artificial baits. Stripers and catfish love eels. And flathead catfish prefer live minnows to any other bait. Even the pickiest trout will readily eat a hellgrammite.

Yellow perch will hit wax worms and mealworms under the ice when they ignore everything else. Trout can be taken on worms and crickets better than on artificial flies and spinners. And the traditional baits for bream are earthworms and crickets.

Options for Saltwater Live Bait

All kinds of saltwater flats fish, including trout and redfish, love shrimp. A live menhaden or mullet will get a trophy tarpon to bite when all else fails. Flounder seem to prefer a live minnow drifted near the bottom to just about any other kind of bait. And surf fishermen catch everything from sea bass to sharks on live minnows.

You'll get more bites if you match the size of your bait to the fish you're after. For fish with small mouths, use smaller bait. And try to match the size of the bait to what the fish normally feed on. This is known as "matching the hatch."

Saltwater stripers love eels just as much as their landlocked freshwater counterparts. Dropping a live squid or minnow to the bottom on a reef will quickly attract the attention of grouper, sea bass, and all the other predators around it. Trolling live bait for big-game fish like sailfish, marlin, and swordfish is the best way to take them. Bluefish eat up whole bloodworms, and croaker and spots in bays eat them up when the worms are cut into bite-size pieces.

How to Keep Bait Alive

Special containers are made for most kinds of live bait, and you should use the right one. Most live bait does better if kept cool and out of the sun. Storing live bait for long periods of time is a lot of trouble so plan on using your bait soon after getting it. It's much better to get fresh live bait for each trip rather than to get a lot and try to keep it for a several days.

Keeping Freshwater Bait Alive

Live earthworms in the refrigerator may not sound too appetizing, but a cool, moist place is the best place to store them. Put the paper cups they're sold in into the refrigerator and they'll last several days. If you dig your own earthworms, put them in a paper cup with a lid — don't use plastic or metal. Paper will allow the soil to breath and not condense too much moisture in it.

Minnows can be kept in an aerated tank or a thirty-gallon plastic trashcan. Put an aquarium aerator in the bottom of the trashcan and the minnows will keep for several weeks. Drop a little goldfish food on top of the water if you plan on keeping them more than a few days. Take a few minnows out to use and leave the rest for later. If you're staying at the lake or have a pond nearby, you can use a minnow bucket with holes in it to let fresh water flow through.

On hot days add a few ice cubes to your minnow bucket to cool the water. Do this all during the day to keep them lively and healthy. Don't add many at one time; if you get the water too cool, they'll die when you put them into the warmer water you're fishing.

Crickets will live a long time in a good wire cricket box. Put a cut potato in the box with them each day for moisture and food. Make sure the box is in the shade, out of direct sunlight. A cricket box with a wide top and a metal sleeve allows you to take out one cricket at a time. You can use it while fishing and to keep them alive between trips. A wire tube with a stopper in one funnel-shaped end also works well, but it's more trouble to get a cricket out when you need it.

For other baitfish, a round bait tank is just about the only way to keep them alive unless you have a dock on the lake and can put a big wire basket in the water for them. While you're fishing from a boat, you can keep them in a bait tank or a thirty-gallon plastic trashcan, but you need to use a twelve-volt aerator or small bilge pump to keep the water circulating. Since most baitfish are open-water fish they need a big tank, and won't survive well in smaller minnow buckets.

Mealworms, wax worms, and grubs kept in a container of meal in the refrigerator will stay alive and healthy for several days. Leeches, salamanders, and hellgrammites can be kept in moist moss in a tightly sealed container with a few air holes. Crayfish need to have shallow containers of water that stays aerated. Wasp nests containing larvae need to be put in a paper sack and kept in the refrigerator, but be real careful when you open it because some may have matured and can sting you.

Make sure everyone in the house knows where you keep your bait in the refrigerator. Don't take a chance that a kid may open a bag with a live wasp in it, or that anyone may open the wrong container looking for a snack.

Prepared Bait

It's often more convenient when going fishing to take along bait that's not alive. There are many kinds of baits that fill the gap between live bait and artificial bait; they're easy to carry and easy to use. Some of them were once alive but others are things fish would never see in their natural world.

Frozen Bait

Many kinds of live bait can be frozen and kept for a later time when you can't get live bait. You can often buy frozen bait cheaply, or you can prepare it yourself. You can freeze the right amount for each trip and keep it a long time until needed. Frozen baits also make good chum.

Chum is bait that's put out to attract fish to an area. Pieces of fish and other bait make good chum and you can freeze them whole and grind them up when needed or grind them up and freeze the chum in containers for later use. Chumming isn't legal in all areas though, so you should check with your local authorities first.

Kinds of Frozen Bait

Just about any kind of minnow or baitfish can be frozen and used later. Freezing them does make them soft and they won't stay on the hook as well as when fresh, but they will work. Freeze whole shiners, small shad, and other small fish in cartons to thaw and use later. If possible freeze the fish separately on a cookie sheet then dump them into a container with a tight top. This allows you to take out a whole minnow without chipping apart a chunk of frozen fish or waiting for the whole block to thaw.

Earthworms don't freeze well at all and you shouldn't bother trying. They're usually fairly easy to find in bait stores, so plan on buying them fresh rather than trying to freeze them.

Bigger baitfish can be frozen whole then cut up after they thaw, or you can cut pieces the size you will use and freeze them like individual minnows. Freezing fish in cartons of water will help them keep in better condition longer but they are harder to use since you have to let the whole block thaw. If you're planning on grinding them up for chum, it doesn't matter whether you freeze them whole or in blocks of ice.

Crayfish can be frozen whole for later use as can frogs, crabs, and salamanders, but they don't work as well when frozen. Clams will work after being frozen and are best if you freeze them in the shell; the shell will open and you can get the meat out easier. Shrimp and squid both freeze well and can be used whole or cut up after thawing. Hellgrammites can be frozen separately and used when thawed, but live ones are better bait.

Crickets, mealworms, wax worms, catalpa worms, and grub worms can all be frozen in a container with corn meal in it. The meal keeps them from sticking together and from becoming mushy when thawed. Catalpa worms are probably the best of the group to use after freezing.

Other soft-bodied baits like sandworms and bloodworms don't freeze well at all. They become mushy after freezing, and the only way you can use them is to put them in net bags. With these and other very mushy baits, cut a small square of net material, such as pantyhose, and wrap the bait it in, tying the top together. Then attach it to the hook inside the net bag. Other baits are better for that purpose. Although they have soft bodies, leeches can be frozen individually and you won't have the problem of them wrapping around the hook as they do when they're fresh. Wasp larvae can be frozen in the nest and used later but they do become softer, and you can't refreeze them.

How to Fish Frozen Bait

Some fish like blue catfish seem to take frozen bait almost as well as live bait. Others such as bass are unlikely to hit bait that's not alive. Flounder and other bottom-feeding saltwater fish will hit frozen bait, and some game fish will hit whole frozen baitfish when trolled or given movement some other way.

Add a small inline spinner in front of your hook to give flash to frozen bait. This will help attract game fish that usually feed on live bait and make frozen bait more appealing.

Since frozen bait often becomes softer, the use of a double or treble hook can help. You don't have to worry about injuring the bait since it is already dead, so use a double or treble hook and stick it into the bait in more than one place. Try to arrange it so it hangs naturally on the hook. You can also use a bait holder rig with two hooks tied together with a short leader. Stick one hook in the head of the frozen bait and the other in the tail to hold it better, or keep it straight in the case of a small frozen minnow.

Frozen bait won't have any action of its own but it works well for bottom feeders that scavenge for food. Rig it on a fish finder rig or a simple sinker and hook, cast it out, and let it sit for catfish in fresh water and grouper in salt water. For fish that prefer a moving bait, drift it on spreader rigs or bait walkers (see Chapter 9 for more on rigs and bait walkers). Tipping a jig with a frozen minnow and casting it will work for walleye and other fish that like movement in their food, too.

Freeze-Dried Bait

You may accidentally freeze-dry baits yourself if you leave some minnows in the freezer too long, but it is better to purchase them. Many kinds of bait ranging from crickets to minnows are freeze-dried and sold in zipper bags. They keep well for a long time and will catch fish, but not as well as fresh-frozen baits. Use them as an emergency supply or when you need lightweight bait.

Freeze-dried baits are the lightest baits you will find so they're good baits to carry when backpacking. They keep for a long period of time, don't take up much space, and are very lightweight, all of which are important factors when backpacking.

Kinds of Freeze-Dried Bait

Minnows are the most popular kinds of freeze-dried baits and many tackle stores sell them. They're often more expensive than live or frozen bait and don't work as well. You may also find crickets, grasshoppers, crayfish, and leeches for fresh water, and clams, squid, shrimp, and crabs for salt water. Look for baits that are whole, not broken apart, and store them so they won't be damaged after you buy them.

How to Fish Freeze-Dried Bait

It's usually best to soak freeze-dried baits in water to soften them before using. Treble and double hooks hold them better than single hooks, and bait holder hooks (hooks with barbs on the shaft or a small spring) may be a good choice. These baits retain the smell of the live bait so they can be effective for fish like catfish that scavenge for food using smell.

Add a small inline spinner to these baits for added attraction, too. They make good jig tippers and can add enough smell and meat to them to make you get more bites. Fishing them under a cork or sitting still on the bottom will get bites from bluegill and other active feeders that eat any kind of food they can find. The ones for salt water work for bottom feeders when dropped down on a fish finder rig but will work better when drifted under a cork or moved along the bottom.

Preserved Bait

Storing bait in brine or some other preservative can make it last a long time and keep it useful. Some baits, like salmon eggs, have to be preserved or they won't last. You can also find some kinds of preserved baits that fish would otherwise never see, like pork rind. Preserved baits are easy to carry and will last practically forever.

Kinds of Preserved Bait

Pickled minnows and frogs can be found in many tackle stores, covered in the preserving fluid and stored in zipper bags or bottles. They stay moist and keep well, and you can take out one bait at a time and use it without damaging the others. When preserved correctly the baits retain their natural colors, or have color added to them to attract fish.

Crayfish, leeches, crabs, worms, and many other kinds of baits can also be found pickled or preserved in some kind of fluid, too. Since the pickling process adds a smell of its own, these baits can be less effective than frozen or freeze-dried baits. If preserved in brine the saltwater baits will not have an added smell and many freshwater fish, like bass, seem to like salty bait, so it may actually help.

Pork rind — the skin and fat of a hog — is a special bait that is cut into strips or chunks and pickled in brine. It's been around for many years and, except for live bait, may be one of the best big bass baits available. Pork rind is cut into thick strips with fat attached to make eel and worm shapes and into chunks with tails for jig trailers. The thin skin is cut into strips for trailers for spinners and spoons.

You can buy salmon eggs, which are preserved in borax, making them tough enough to stay on an egg holder hook. Eggs would dry out quickly if not preserved and would be so soft they wouldn't stay on the hook. Eggs can also be dyed different colors for an added attraction for fish.

Fish tend to swallow prepared baits, making hook removal difficult. If you're planning on catching and releasing, it's best to avoid baits like salmon eggs, which fish swallow so deeply you can't remove the hook without injuring them.

How to Fish Preserved Bait

The "jig and pig" of bass fishing gets its name from a jig tipped with a pork frog, a chunk of pork skin and fat pickled in brine. Pickled pork is cut into chunks with tails on them that wave like crayfish arms when fished behind a jig. Pork chunks can be dyed different colors and have been known to catch a huge number of big bass. Although plastic chunks have replaced them in many cases, pork still works best in cold water and gives something extra that plastic can't match.

A small strip of white pork rind added to a small spinner is deadly for bream and other panfish. The little strip waves enticingly as you reel the spinner through the water. Put a long strip behind a spoon and swim it through grass beds and lily pads for pike and bass.

Drifting a salmon egg in a stream is one of the best ways to catch trout. It's a very natural bait that trout naturally feed on and it's hard to beat. And unlike natural eggs, preserved ones can be dyed different colors to show up better in different colored water and to attract fish under a wide variety of conditions. In some trout streams, eggs aren't allowed, so check regulations before using them.

Other pickled and preserved baits are just like frozen baits because they work best for bottom feeders that find their food by scent. You can hook these baits to jigs or put a small spinner ahead of them for added flash to attract fish. And they often stay on the hook well since the pickling process sometimes makes them very tough.

Tools and Techniques

This section will cover all of your basic tools and techniques for getting out on the water and catching a fish. I want to be very clear that I am looking to offer a setup here that can work in most any water and catch some type of fish there. The reason I am saying this is because this rig will be very basic but will allow you to catch a variety of fish from almost any body of water, and for a beginner, this is what you will want.

The tools will be the hardware that it will take to be prepared for your fishing adventure. We will cover things like rods, reels, lines, pliers, cutters, tackle boxes and hats, among other items. This section will ensure that when you pull up to your new fishing spot you will have what you need to catch a fish and take it off the hook successfully

The techniques section will be a little broader. There will be some very important techniques covered in this section that you will have to be able to understand before success is achieved on the water. We will be all over the place in the techniques section but I will teach you how to cast, how to tie on a hook, jigging, and using floats, to name a few.

Tools

The Open Faced Reel

My recommendation on reel type for the beginner is the open faced reel. I have used it all my life and it is just the best. There are people who are in love with bait casting reels but the open faced reel gives an incredible degree of access. This access is important to deal with things like loops and tangles that can happen throughout the fishing day.

As you can see in the accompanying picture you have the spool which contains all of your fishing line. It is important to keep this spool full and ready to go with fresh line. Change your line at least annually.

Above the spool is your drag. You will be able to turn your drag clockwise to tighten it or counter to loosen it. I guess to understand what that means you will need a brief description of what the drag is capable of. Your drag dictates how much tension is allowed on the line before the spool turns and gives more line. If you are after big fish you will be looking to have a drag with some give so when that big boy goes on a run it won't snap your line.

The bail is the small golden half ring that surrounds the spool. The bail controls the mechanism that allows your line to stay taut while you reel it and jerk it. When you flip this bail your line will come off the spool liberally. You will flip the bail before you cast.

The handle of the reel is where you will take control of the line and how fast or slow it is retrieved. This is also how you will reel in your catch. Some reels have a button on the bottom that allows you to back crank or reel in the opposite direction. Some people utilize this as a method to fight big fish. For me this back crank just tends to give me loops and tangles so I avoid it.

Floats

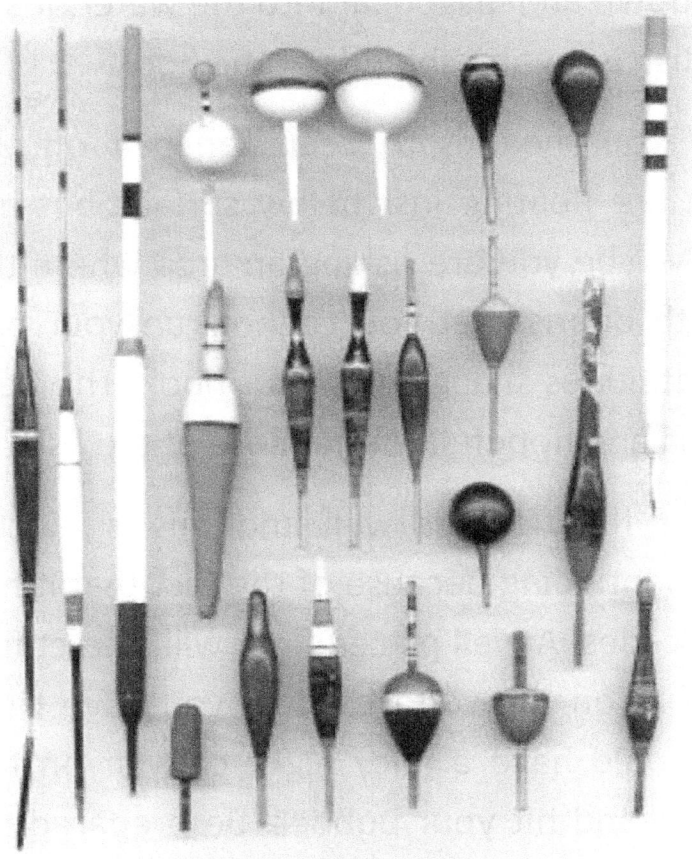

If you are going to be using live bait in any capacity you better stock up on some sort of floats. There are quite a few varieties to choose from. This shouldn't intimidate you. Instead you need to consider what we talked about in the early chapter about knowing your quarry.

Your float or bobber has two purposes in its use; the first being an indicator of when a fish has started to peck at your bait. When this happens the bobber will dance around and, well, bob up and down. If the fish has a good hold on whatever you have on the hook the bobber will go down and disappear into the water. It's at this point you know the fish is on and should set the hook.

The second purpose of your float is to keep the bait off the bottom. Maybe the fish are floating just below surface but not feeding on the surface. Maybe you are fishing an area where the bottom is so riddled with debris that you cannot run your bait through it for fear of continuous snagging of your hook. The float keeps your bait in set area and hopefully in the nose of the fish.

There is another use for the float as well and this is a little sardonic but it is worth mentioning because of the fact that it has plagued my family for decades. A well placed float will attract fish and they will hit your float on the surface when you have tried every other tactic. You could have a juicy night crawler on the hook and a fish will come and hit your bobber. Be prepared for the laughs to follow.

Forceps

These are essential for safely removing hooks from the mouths of fish. When you are dealing with a riled up game fish with treble hooks in its mouth it's important that you have a tool to grab those hooks that are stuck and avoid those hooks that aren't yet stuck. You do not want a hook in you passed the barb and also have it attached to a live fish. There are upper levels of the human capacity for pain and flailing fish digging a hook deep into your flesh ranks up there.

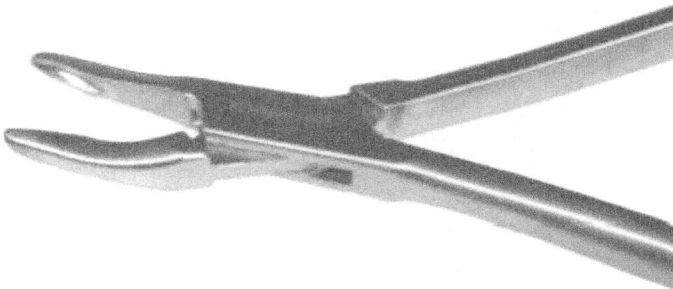

It's easy to get deep into the mouth of a fish in ways that your fingers just cannot. Of course these have a variety of other uses but most importantly they will keep you safe. Don't head out on the water without them.

Techniques

Tie on a hook

The step by step process for the knot needed to tie on a hook will follow in the set of pictures. This knot has held up through so many of my fishing adventures. I challenge you to find and easier and more effective knot. Trust me there are so many out there that you just might. This knot, however, has been handed down in my family and is just the way it's done.

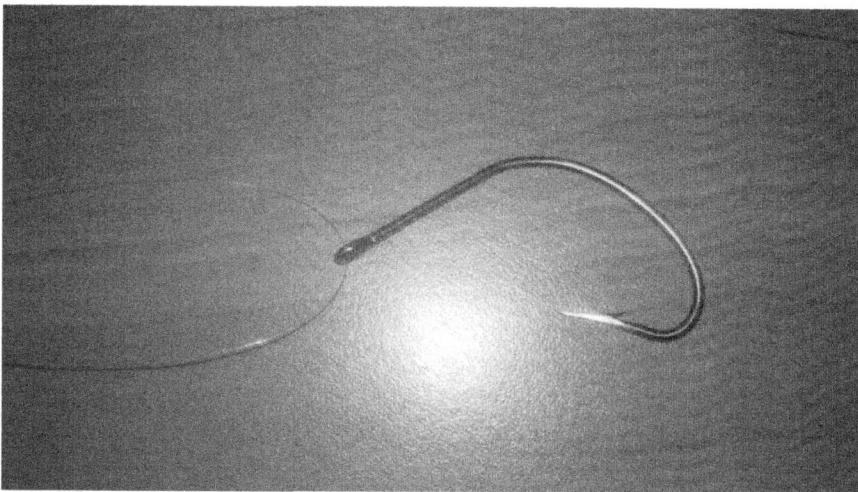

Begin by threading the line through the eye of your hook.

Create a big loop with the line. You have several hundred yards of line on your spool. Don't be stingy when using it. It's much easier to tie a knot with plenty of line.

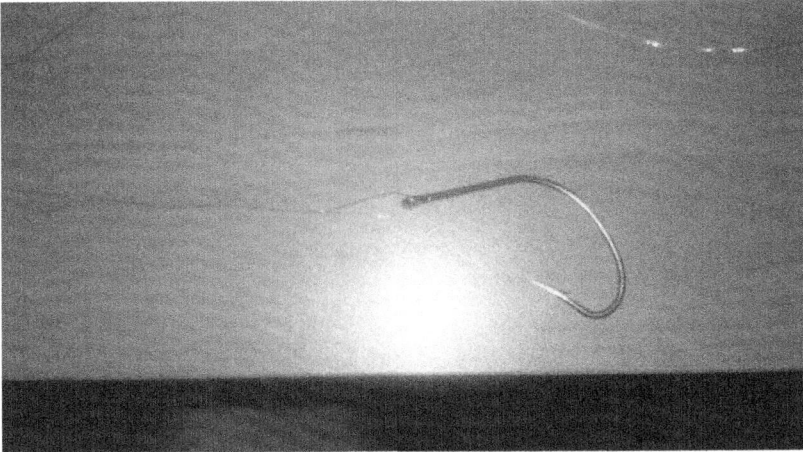

Twist the hook seven times for luck and of course for strength.

Take the end of your line put it through the original loop

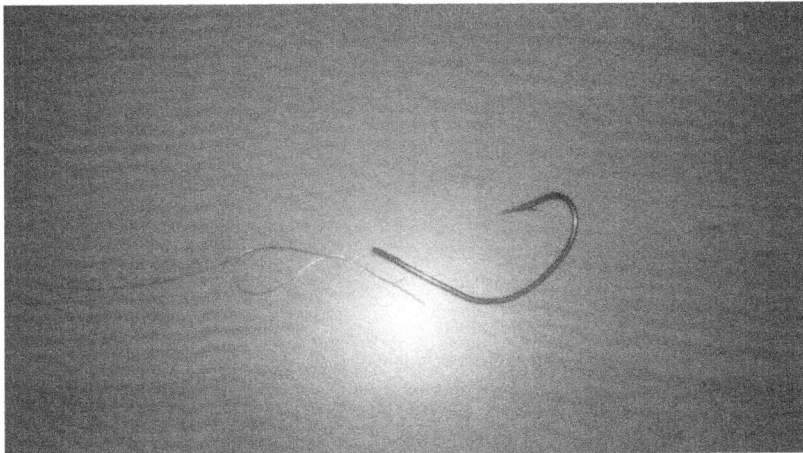

Run it back up through the new loop created

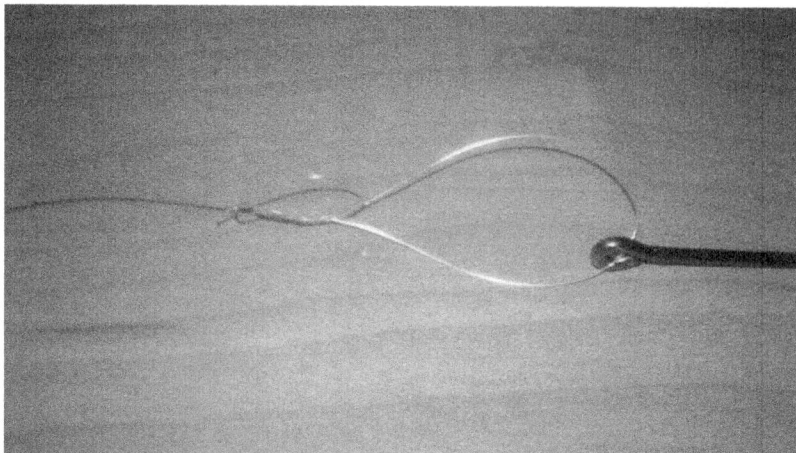

Slowly tighten down the knot and you can even use some saliva to help it along its way.

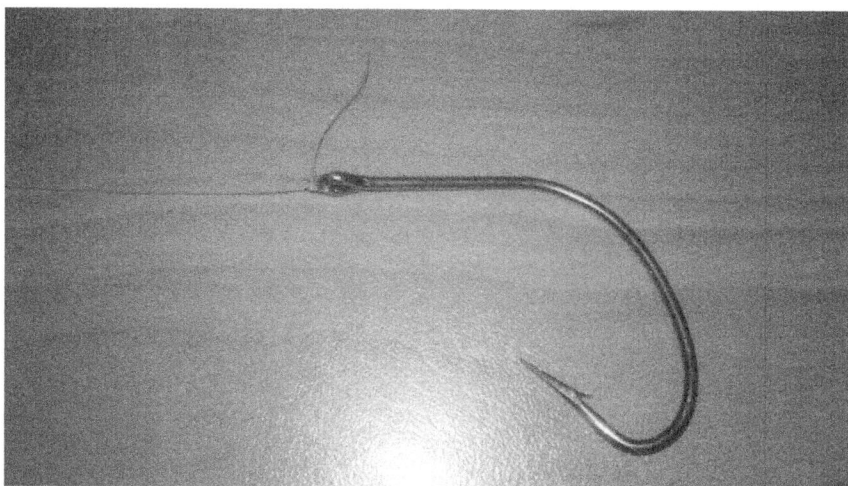

Tighten up against the eye of the hook and you are ready to go!

Casting

Absolutely one of the most crucial elements of fishing is the cast. You must he able to place bait or lure right where the fish will see it. Casting will take time to master. It's important to be able to cast under hanging tree limbs or into small pools deep behind cover. Your accuracy is all when it comes to casting. There will be more on this later. For now we will discuss the basics of casting.

Reel your bait up till there is about 6 inches of line hanging from the last guide on your rod. Hold the line with your index finger and flip the bail. This will allow the line to come freely off the spool. If you let go of the line at this point your bait will merely fall to the ground.

Now, using your head as 12 O'clock, drop the rod and the hanging bait behind you to about 2 O'clock. Quickly whip the rod forward and release your index finger from holding the line when your rod hits 11 O'clock. This should send your lure or bait flying. Now modify form here based on where the bait falls.

An earlier release will send your bait further up and usually leads to more length where as a later release will work into a shorter cast that could be used for greater accuracy. There are many ways to modify your cast but the best way to get better is to keep at it.

Jigging

There is no other fishing technique that has netted me more fish than this method of slowly bouncing weighted artificial bait off the bottom of a stream or pond. Jigging is an art form that requires some practice but it most certainly pays off.

The first thing you must-do if you want to become proficient at the technique is to learn to feel the bottom of the water you are fishing. This starts by casting weighted artificial bait into the pond or stream and allowing it time to hit bottom. Next begin to reel it back in, slowly slowly! As it makes its way back to you there will be resistance either in the form of the bait running over rocks, through weeds or logs under the water. When you feel this resistance give your rod tip a slight jerk up. This should pop the bait over this type of cover. Once the resistance is gone continue slowly reeling again.

In the beginning you will get hooked on the bottom and lose hooks and bait that get wedged under rocks or into logs. This is part of learning. You will know you are jigging right if you occasionally get hung on the bottom. Don't be discouraged.

This method of running a bait right along the bottom drives fish insane. It's not easy to replicate and quite frankly is so natural that fish can't resist it. If you can master this technique you will increase the likelihood of success exponentially

Reading Water

What do you see when you look at a body of water? Does it appear to you a just a hollowed out portion of the earth with water running through it? Does anything stand out to you about this area you are fishing? These are crucial questions to ask oneself in the early stages of fishing. If you cast into every lake or stream and picture a smooth cement swimming pool bottom than you are lost from the start.

Creeks, rivers and ponds though full of water all have an underwater landscape. There may be boulders, sunken trees or underwater vegetation. Each of the previous mentioned habitats provides incredible cover both for hiding and feeding. Knowing what lies beneath is the most important part of fishing the bottom.

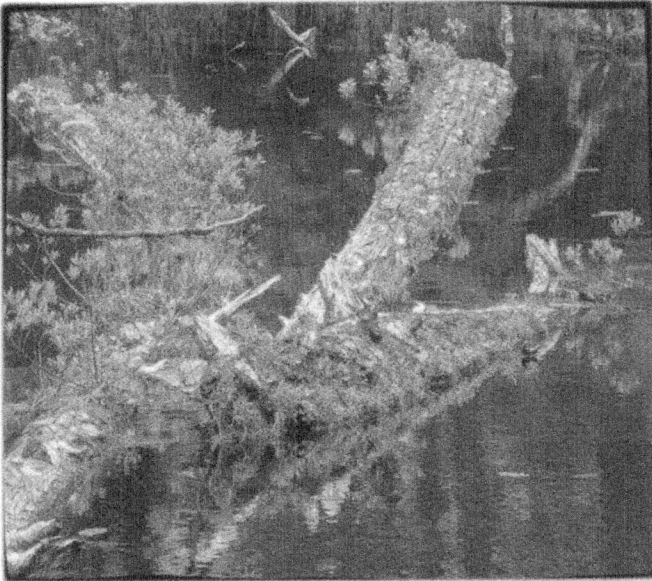

Sunken Trees or Logs

Sunken trees and logs are the perfect spot for fish to hide. These provide shade on hot days for these cold blooded creatures and protection from other predators. If you find one of these gems covered in moss with turtles walking on top of it take a shot underneath and you will more than likely get success.

Large Boulder

Fish in rivers and streams are fighting current all day every day. There is no greater rest for them than that of a large boulder that cuts the water. Behind these boulders fish will lay eggs, rest or just set up shop for the next unlucky food that was taken away by the current. This is the number one hiding spot of the smallmouth bass.

When I am fishing large boulders I prefer to drop jigs or plastic worms and baits that sink just behind them where the water is breaking and allows the current to rush the bait over to the slack side. I know there are fish lurking back there and most times they come out and say hi.

Weed Growth

There is a certain point in the summer when large mats of grasses and weeds start to form on the surface of slow moving waters. These weeds or weed beds are havens for summer species for many reasons. They provide several resources to fish in one tight spot. If you work the edges of these beds or even bust into them with a heavy jig the fish will be there waiting.

Remember, fish are cold blooded creatures so they cannot regulate their body temperature. In the dog days of summer, they have to seek out cover or be slow cooked by the magnified rays of sun coming through the water. Weeds provide an impenetrable cover.

You also want to know these conditions and others affect the water flow. For example, large boulders will create slack or slow water behind them. This is area is perfect for a fish to rest outside of the current and pick off easy food as it blows by. That makes it a perfect area to cast as well.

Bodies of water also create their own fishing holes that you have to learn to identify. All of these areas will hold fish as well.

This picture of the beautiful James River in Alberta is an incredible shot of the above mentioned features of a river. Each of these should be fished and observed during an outing. These are naturally occurring conditions in a body of water that allow you to pinpoint areas where fish might be hiding. Understanding each and the why's of a fish's being there will allow you to become a master at reading water.

Just beyond the fallen tree and the rocks on the left side of the bank you see a smooth portion of water that hugs the bank. It seems to be slack water that almost cuts back into the bank. This area is called an eddy. Like the boulder we discussed above these eddies are much easier areas to rest and attack from. Fish an eddy by throwing the water just above it and allow it to flow down into the eddy.

The riffles or fast water that flows down the center of this picture are great for fish to lie in particularly in the summer. These hot months sap oxygen from the water and often times make it hard on fish to survive. As the water rushes over rocks it creates oxygen and the cools the water as well. This tradeoff is often times worth it for the fish as they also get food funneled through the riffles as well.

Beyond the riffles there will be something I call the bubble line. The bubble line will always contain fish. It usually forms below dams or fast moving waters. This slow line of bubbles and floating debris will follow a unique path and within that patch picky fish will look up to procure some food from that line. The bubbles often flow to an eddy and the cycle continues. Fish the bubble line by either shooting right into it or by casting your bait just to the side of the bubble line. This should net you something worth talking about.

Another important aspect of reading a body of water is to understand the difference between upstream and downstream. These two terms explain the directional flow of the water in a river or stream. Each flow has perks for the types of fishing you are doing.

Downstream explains the direction of the water as it flows towards the mouth of the river. If you are moving in the direction that the water is flowing then you are headed downstream.

This is a great option when you are taking long casts and allowing your bait to go further downstream. Fishing under dams is a great example of this. The trouble is fish are facing upstream and see you coming. They will see the dust clouds you kick up and your physical body wading toward them. That doesn't mean necessarily that you will be unsuccessful but a big fish will take off into hiding.

Upstream is the direction that leads you up towards the mouth of your body of water. When you are heading against the current you are moving upstream. This is the more arduous a task but adds a level of stealth to your approach that does not exist fishing downstream. I prefer to attack big fish from coming upstream and sneaking along the banks. This eliminates any wakes you make in the water or any dust you kick up while wading through the water.

The final step in reading a body of water is to look over what other types of life are flourishing on the water other than the fish you are after. At any moment there are a number of species of insects, crustaceans and baitfish cruising around in the water as well. The location and behavior of these species will determine a lot about where your fish may be hiding as well.

In the summer you may happen upon something know as a Trico hatch. This is an event that usually happens in the first rays of sunlight. Trico's are small flying insects that emerge from the water to mate in the sky and die. Very short and interesting life but that's what they do.

During a Trico hatch batfishes go into a feeding frenzy. They all come close to the hatch and eat the falling easy Pickens. If the batfishes follow the Trico's than what do you thing follows the baitfish? Big fish will always be around the Trico hatch

So as you can see there is much more to your average body of water than meets the eye. It's important to understand all the aspects of what you are looking at and how they will affect your efforts. There is no greater skill when it comes to fishing success then understanding the conditions and the makeup of your local body of water.

When To Fish

EARLY SEASON FISHING

After the first warming trends of spring, just after ice-out (in March or April), try some of the following tips.

WHEN TO FISH

The time of day for early season fishing is critical for the best results. The following illustrations can be used as a general rule.

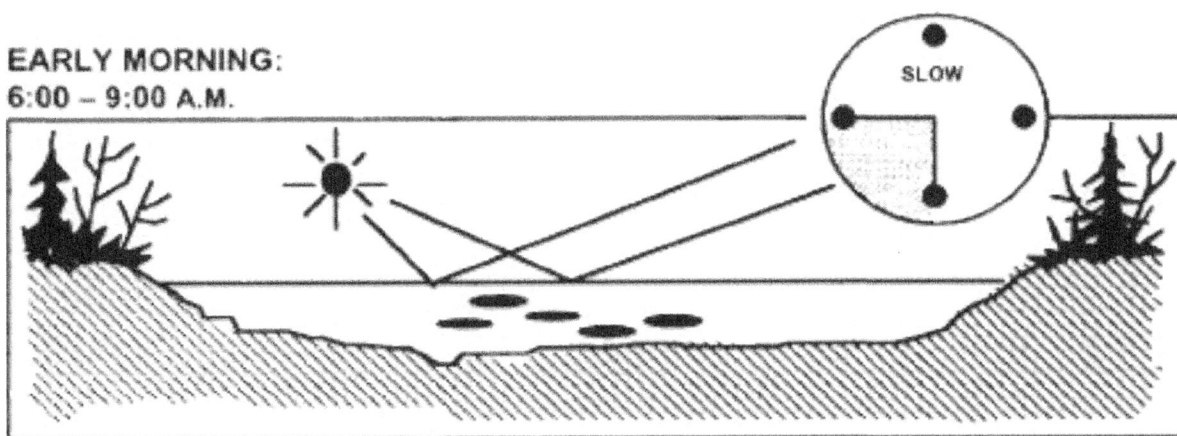

EARLY MORNING:
6:00 – 9:00 A.M.

SLOW

Cool water temperature and low angle of the sun's rays, which bounce off the water, provide little action.

LATE MORNING TO EARLY AFTERNOON:
9:00 A.M. – 1:00 P.M.

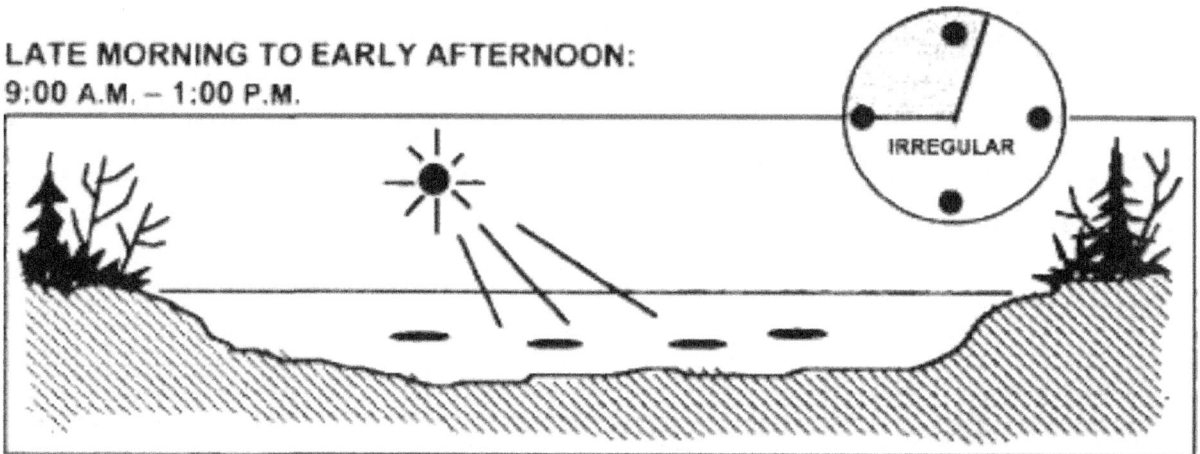

IRREGULAR

Sun starts to penetrate water, surface starts to warm up. Often produces, but could be irregular.

AFTERNOON TO EARLY DUSK:
1:00 – 5:00 P.M.

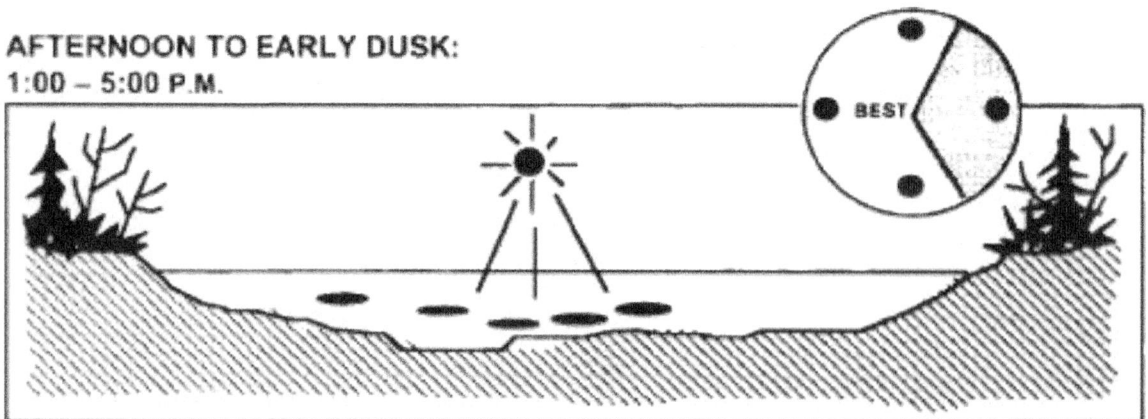

BEST

Sun's rays at maximum penetration. Best time to fish, when air and water temperatures are warmest.

COLD FRONTS

During the early season, cold fronts are one of the key factors that will affect fishing. After a warming trend has set in for a few days and a cold front approaches, the effects of the front are usually as follows:

First day of warming trend

Excellent fishing for a couple of hours during the warmest part of the day. 1:00 to 3:00 P.M.

Second day of warming trend

Excellent fishing same as first day except for a longer period of time. 12:00 to 4:00 P.M.

Third day of warming trend

Good fishing in the late morning as well as in the afternoon. 9:00 A.M. to 4:00 P.M.

Fourth day – Cold front to hit mid-day

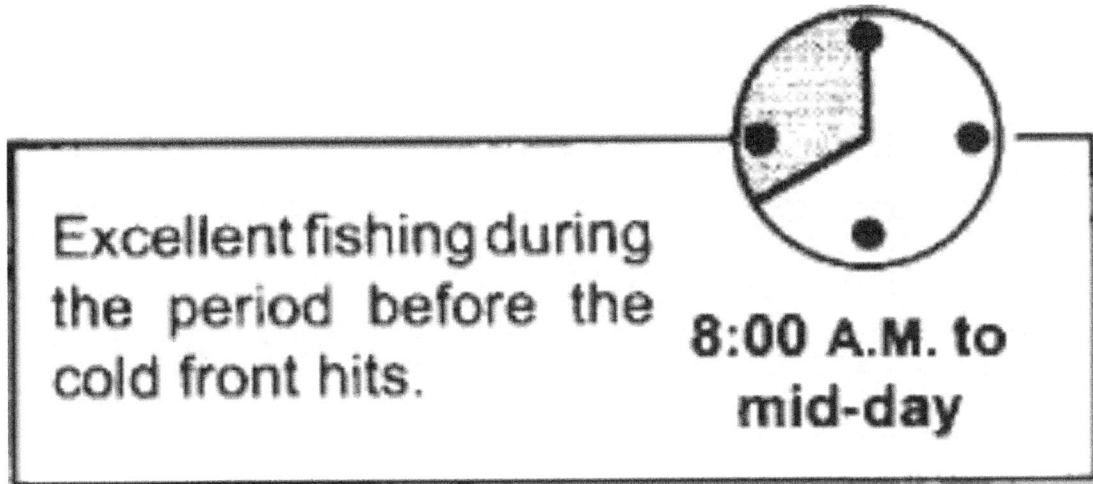

Excellent fishing during the period before the cold front hits.

8:00 A.M. to mid-day

After the cold front hits, fishing will drop off or come to a complete stop. The cycle will repeat itself with the next warming trend and keep repeating until the spring turnover of the lake water.

Knowing where to fish after early season ice-out can be determined by using a little common sense. Consider the following factors when selecting the water you plan to fish.

BEST PLACES

- SMALL LAKES
- PONDS
- QUARRIES

BEST WATER

Remember, darker bottom areas such as mud flats and shallow, silt-covered areas absorb heat and warm up quicker than light-bottomed areas such as sand or gravel. Most early season fish will seek out the warmest water.

HOW TO FISH

Smaller lures or live baits will generally produce best in early spring, as will a slow-to-medium retrieve.

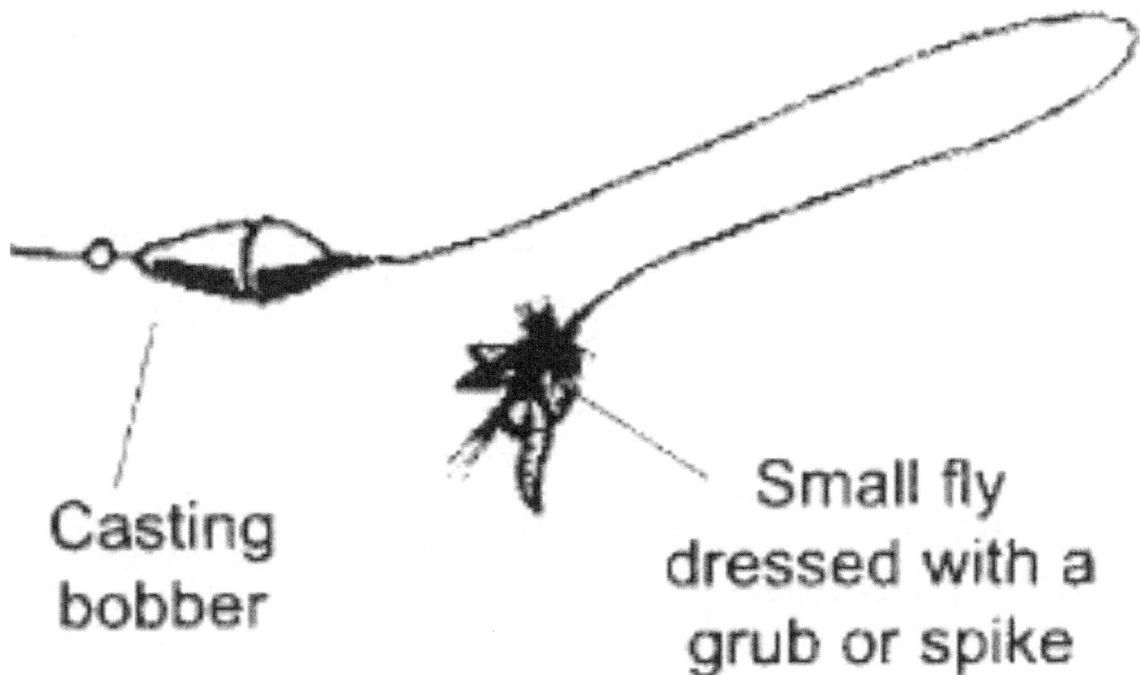

Casting bobber

Small fly dressed with a grub or spike

MID-SEASON FISHING

Here are just a few tips to try during the summer months (mid-June through mid-September) when the fishing slows down.

WHEN TO FISH

During the summer, as a general rule, early morning and late evening are the best times to fish.

EARLY MORNING: 4:30 to 9:00 A.M.

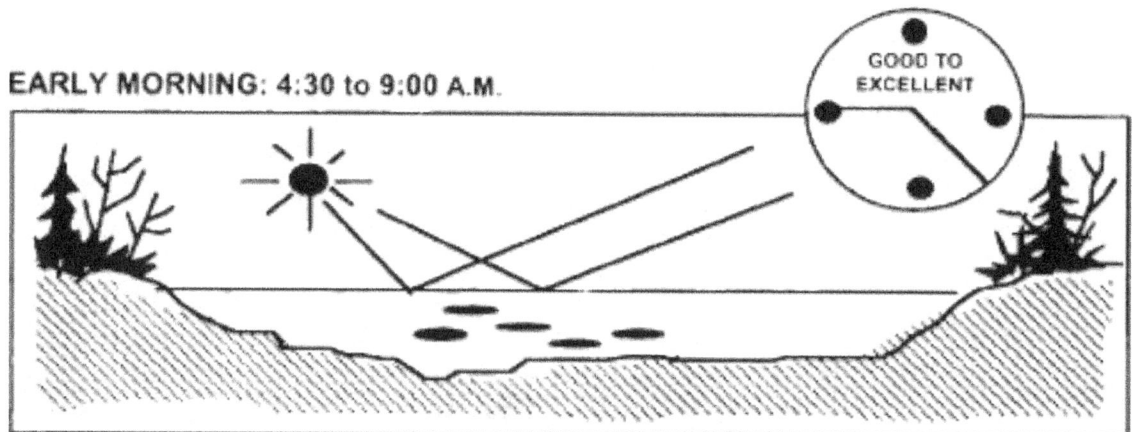

Fish are active just before daybreak (4:30 A.M.) up to about 9:00 A.M. Fishing will be excellent.

MID-MORNING TO LATE AFTERNOON:
9:00 A.M. to 5:00 P.M.

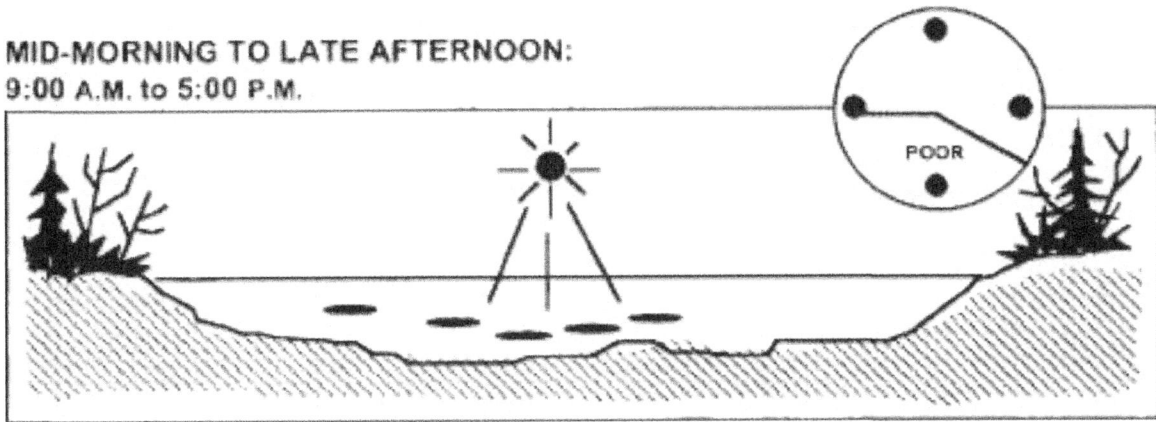

Fish are inactive during most of the day (9:00 A.M. to 5:00 P.M.). Most species will be in deep water.

SUNSET TO EARLY EVENING:
6:00 P.M. to 9:00 P.M.

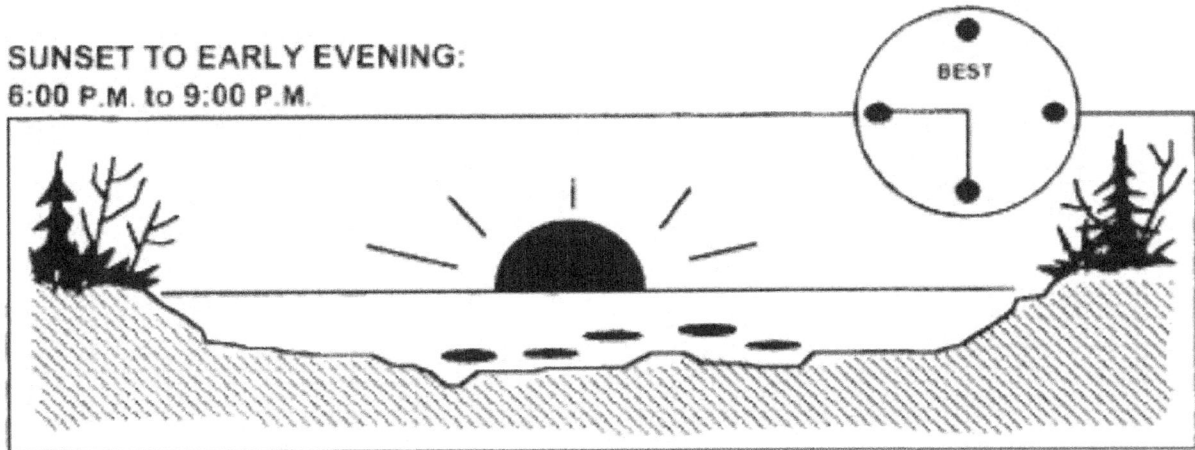

Fish are again active when the sun starts to set (6:00 P.M. to 9:00 P.M.). Excellent fishing.

During the summer months, fish are harder to catch for two main reasons.

THE FOOD CHAIN IS AT ITS PEAK.

Fish become very selective. They feed less often, but gorge themselves when they do start feeding.

FISH ARE HARDER TO FIND DUE TO ABUNDANT COVER.

Weed growth is at its maximum in the summer, and most predators hide in ambush in the weed beds or at their edges. They also use them as resting places between feeding sprees.

SUMMER STAGNATION

During mid-season, most lakes go through what is called the summer stagnation cycle. The surface water warms to well over 39.2° F. and floats on the heavier water below. Most lakes stratify into three layers, as shown below. The top layer is the warmest, the second is cooler and the third is cold and low in oxygen. Most fish species prefer the middle layer, but they all venture into the upper layer during feeding sprees.

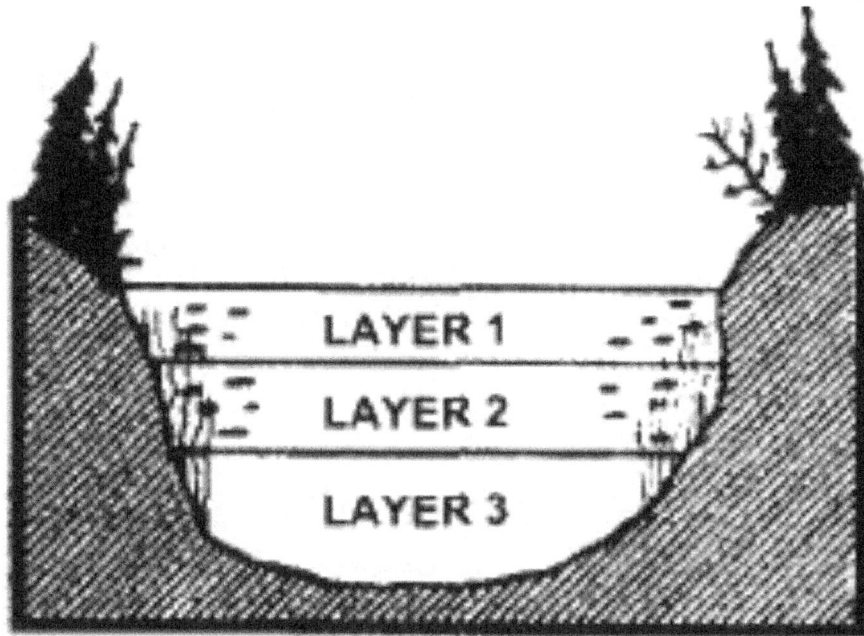

WIND EFFECT

Wind can matter during the hot days of mid-season fishing. Strong winds can push cooler offshore water close in to shore, bringing in bait fish and predators to feed. The bait fish will be attracted to insects blown into the water by the wind, which in turn will attract the larger predators.

The next time you're tempted to fish the calm side of the lake where you may be more comfortable, remember that you may have better luck on the windy side.

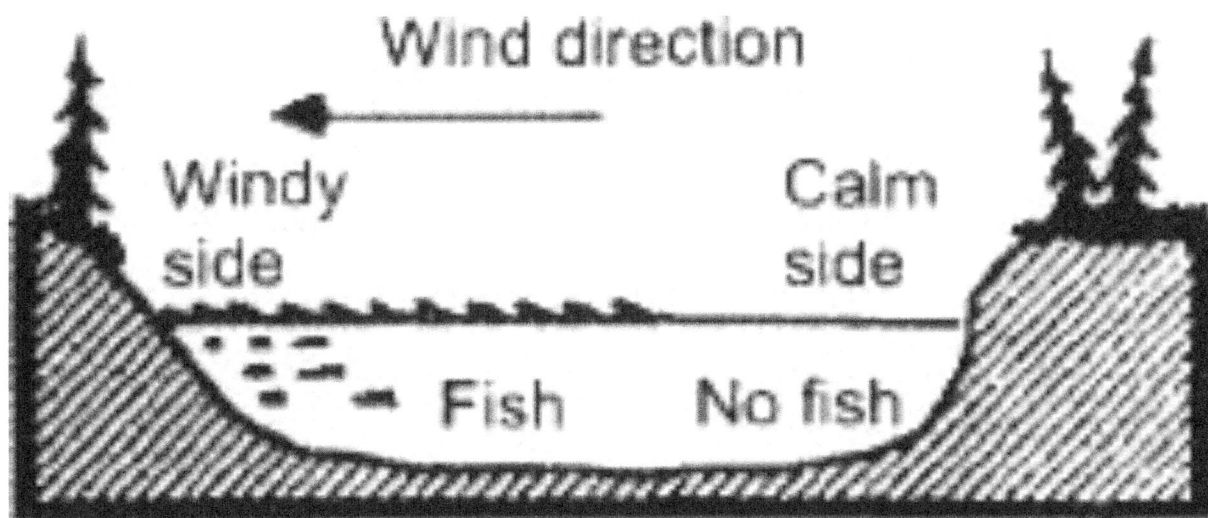

LATE SEASON FISHING

The following are just a few tips to try during the fall months (late September through ice-up), when the fall turnover is in process.

WHEN TO FISH

Water temperature is the most important factor to consider during this period. Daylight hours are shorter, limiting the warming effects of the sun. Conditions will be similar to early spring fishing. As a general rule, most fish will be scattered throughout the lake, feeding near the surface.

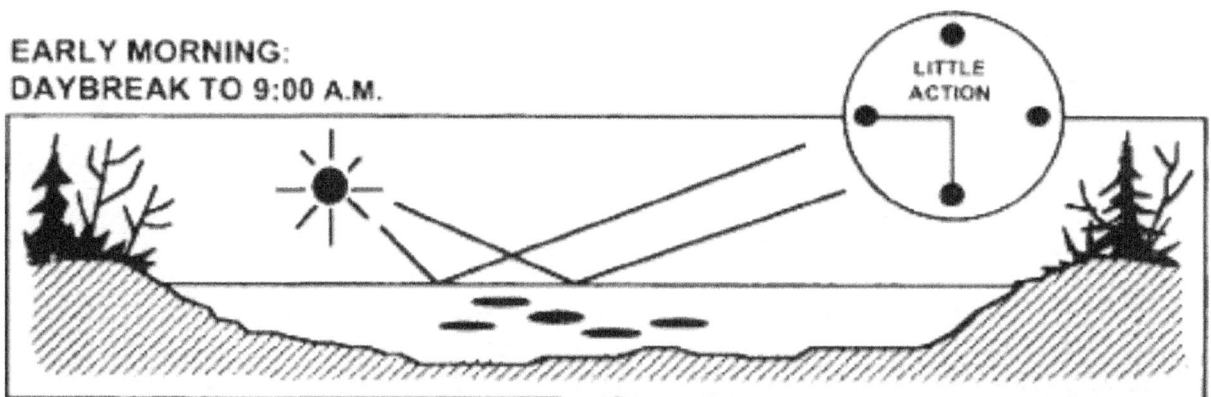

EARLY MORNING:
DAYBREAK TO 9:00 A.M.

LITTLE ACTION

Cool water temperature and little sun penetration into water results in poor action.

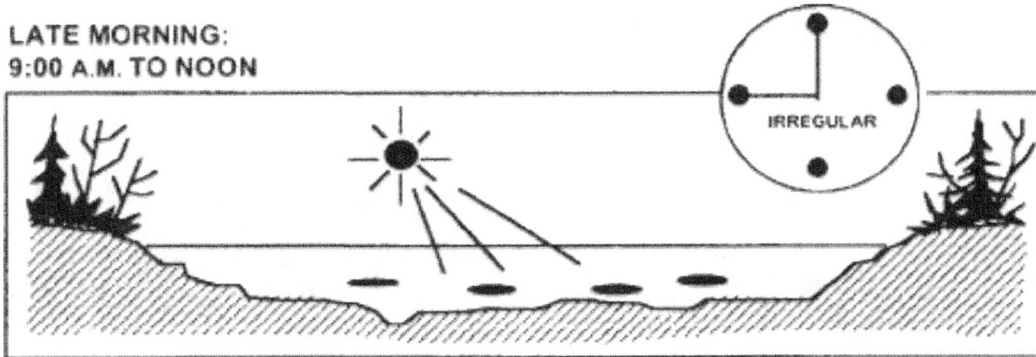

LATE MORNING:
9:00 A.M. TO NOON

IRREGULAR

Fish are active in shallow warmer water. Often produces, but fishing is irregular.

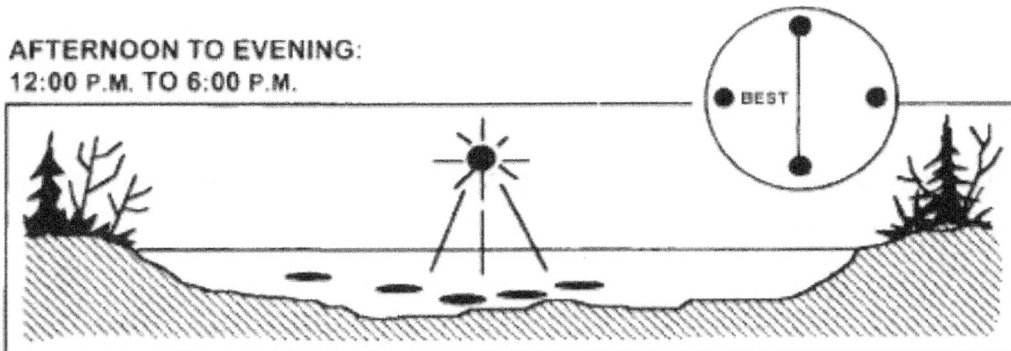

AFTERNOON TO EVENING:
12:00 P.M. TO 6:00 P.M.

BEST

Surface waters are the warmest, and fish are active, including deep water species. Best fishing.

During the fall season, fish become more active. They feed more often and migrate away from their summer haunts.

CONCENTRATIONS OF BAIT FISH

To find active fish consistently in the fall, fish areas having concentrations of bait fish.

WARMEST WATER

Heat from the sun will be the single most important factor that governs fish activity on most lakes in the fall. Fish will seek the warmer surface waters or the shallows.

FALL TURNOVER

During the fall season, the surface water cools until it becomes heavier than the water beneath it. It sinks and mixes with the deeper water until all the water has the same temperature. This process will continue until ice-up and most fish will be scattered throughout the lake, feeding near the surface.

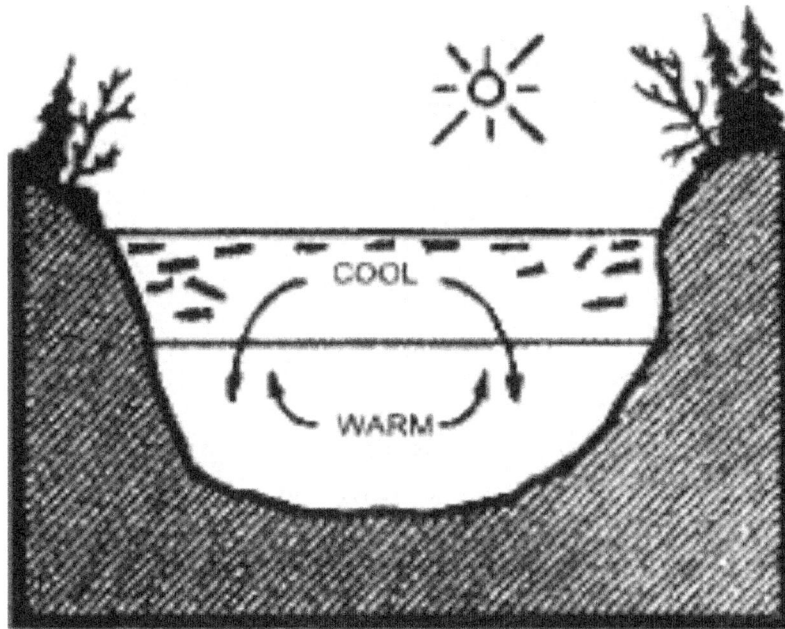

BEST WATERS

As is true in the spring, darker bottom areas such as mud flats or silt-covered areas will attract more fish because they absorb heat and warm the water around them.

■ ■■■

During the late fall season, fish continue to feed much better in very clear water.

■ ■ ■■

When fishing around the time of fall turnover, be willing to change lakes. Some lakes have longer turnover periods than others.

SEASONAL TIPS ON PRESENTATION

The way in which you present your lure or bait during the various seasons can be an important factor. Presentation can be defined as the way you display your bait or lure to a fish. It can include depth, size, color, speed, and action. With each of these factors in mind, consider the following tips to improve your ability to catch fish.

DEPTH

Try the bottom, disturbing it with your bait or lure. Bounce it along, and if that doesn't work, raise it off the bottom and jig it. Vary your depth until you locate the fish. Fish can be found suspended over holes or other forms of structure during any season.

SIZE

Choose the proper size lures for the type of fish you're after. During early spring, smaller lures are more effective.

COLOR

An old rule that's been around for ages regarding color is the one about dark lures on dark days and bright lures on bright days. There may be some truth to the rule, but water clarity should be the most important deciding factor when selecting the color of the lure to be used.

In dirty water, most fish feed by sound or smell because visibility is limited. Brightly colored lures that generate some form of sound would be the most productive under these conditions. In clear water, where visibility is good, bright lures that can be seen readily are your best bet.

SPEED

Another old rule is the one about how fast you retrieve a lure in the early spring.

The rule says "a slow or medium retrieve is the most productive" because in the early spring, when the water is cold, the fish are less active. In most cases this is true, but it's a good practice to vary your retrieves until you discover the one that's the most effective regardless of the season.

ACTION

Another important factor to consider is the action of your bait or lure. All lures represent some type of food on which fish feed. The lure's movement through the water attracts the fish. Try stop-and-go movements, short jerks, side-to-side movements, and the like.

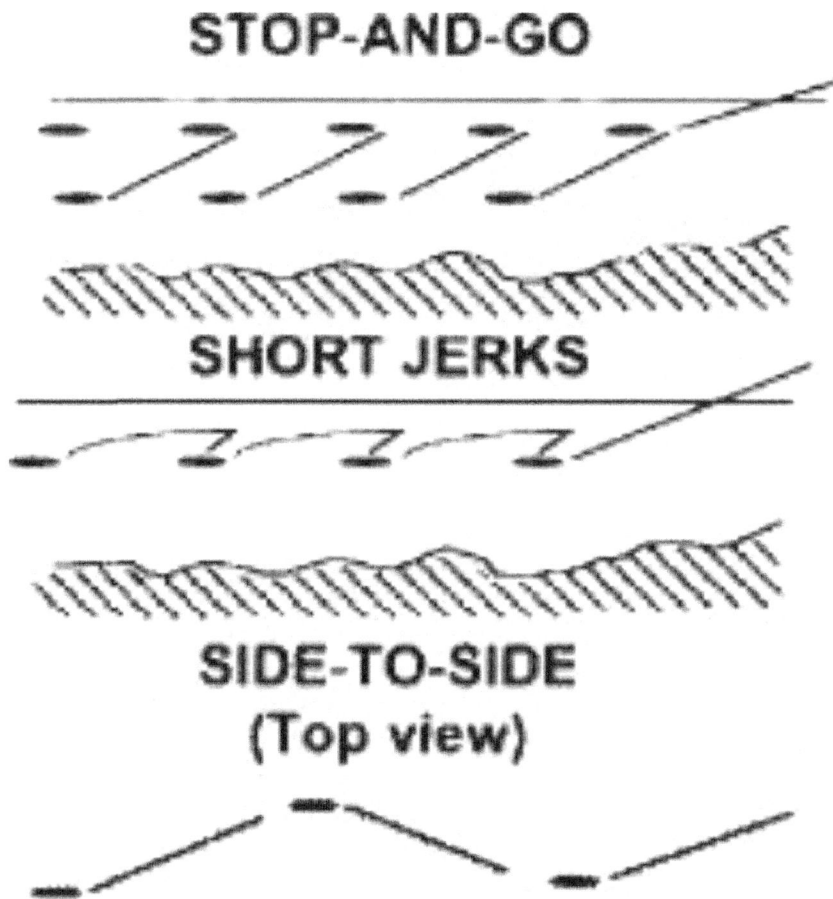

STOP-AND-GO

SHORT JERKS

SIDE-TO-SIDE
(Top view)

SEASONAL LAKE TURNOVERS

A body of water goes through an annual cycle of temperature changes paralleling the seasons. Knowing what the water conditions are and how they affect the fish during each season change can improve your chances of a better catch. The following illustrations depict each season change and the effects on the fish.

SPRING TURNOVER

After ice-out, surface water warms from 32° F to its maximum density at 39° F. The heavier surface waters then sink and mix with the deeper, lighter waters. As the stagnant deep water reaches the surface, it is charged with oxygen by the spring winds and warmed by the sun, repeating the cycle until the water temperature is uniform throughout the lake.

Most fish will be found in the shallower areas of the lake where the waters warm more quickly.

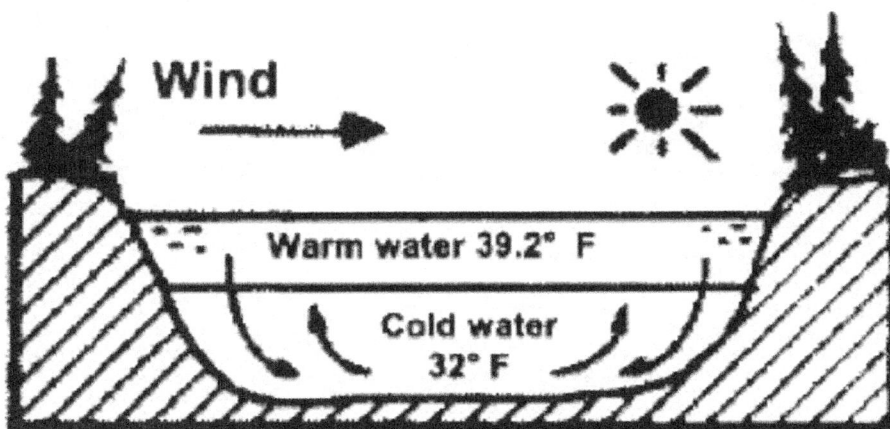

SUMMER STAGNATION

During the summer, surface water warms and rapidly becomes less dense than the water below it. It floats on top of the colder water throughout the entire summer without mixing with the deeper waters. The upper layer of water will vary between 2 and 10 feet in depth, depending on the size of the lake.

Most fish will be found just below the warm surface band of water.

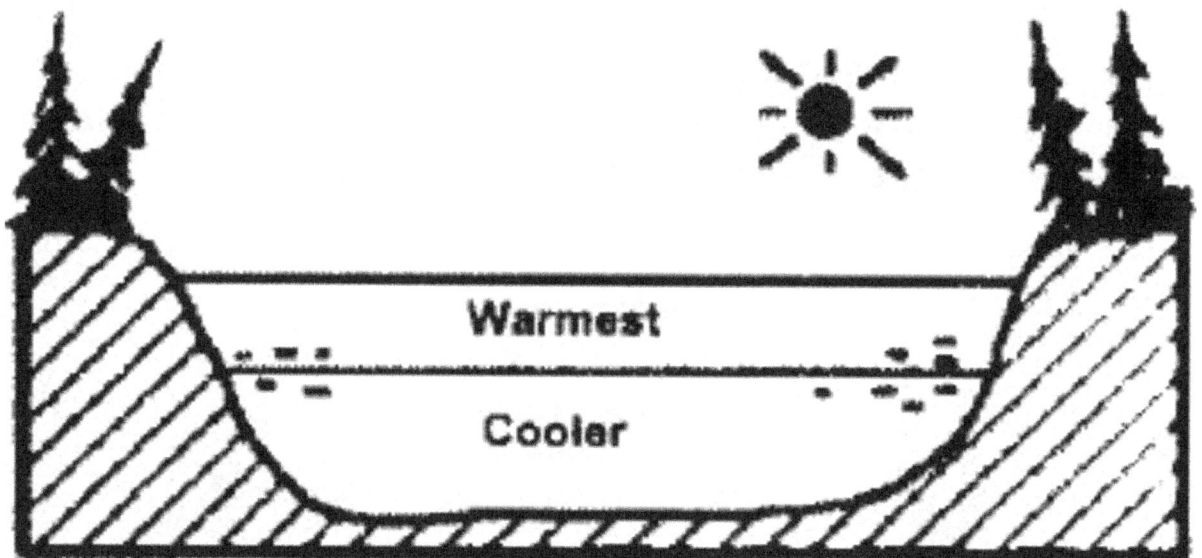

FALL TURNOVER

In the fall season, the surface water cools until it approaches the temperature of the lower water beneath it. When it cools and becomes heavier, it sinks and mixes with the deeper waters until all the water has the same temperature. This process continues until the water reaches 32° F or freezes up.

During this cooling period, most fish will be scattered throughout the lake.

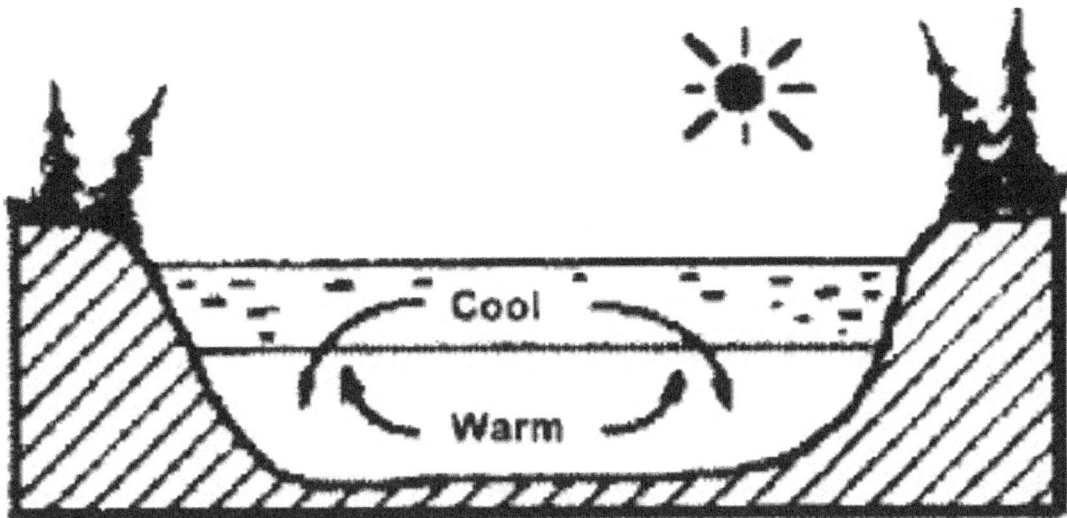

FISHING BY DEGREES

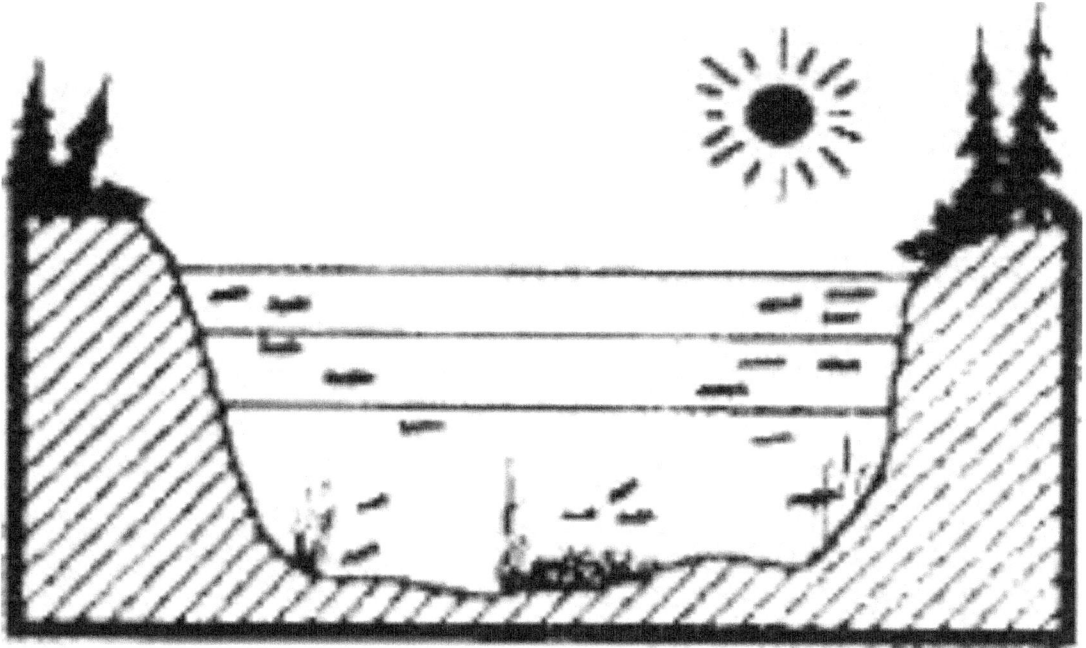

The following chart shows the temperature that specific species of fish prefer. Although you may not find the exact water temperature, most fish will be found in the water closest to the temperature listed on the chart below.

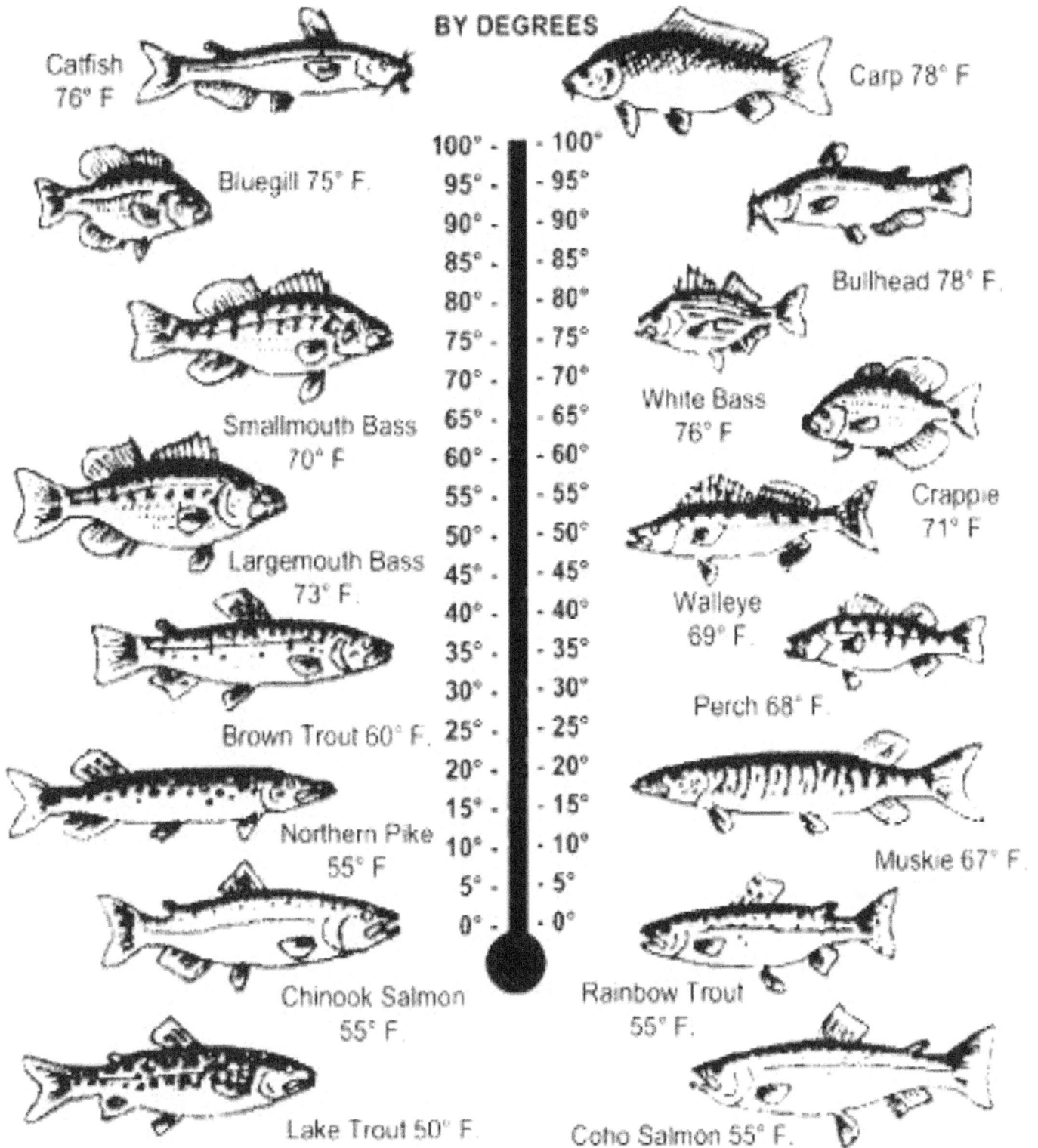

BY DEGREES

Catfish 76° F

Carp 78° F

Bluegill 75° F.

Bullhead 78° F.

100° -	- 100°
95° -	- 95°
90° -	- 90°
85° -	- 85°
80° -	- 80°
75° -	- 75°
70° -	- 70°
65° -	- 65°
60° -	- 60°
55° -	- 55°
50° -	- 50°
45° -	- 45°
40° -	- 40°
35° -	- 35°
30° -	- 30°
25° -	- 25°
20° -	- 20°
15° -	- 15°
10° -	- 10°
5° -	- 5°
0° -	- 0°

Smallmouth Bass 70° F

White Bass 76° F

Largemouth Bass 73° F.

Crappie 71° F

Walleye 69° F.

Brown Trout 60° F.

Perch 68° F.

Northern Pike 55° F

Muskie 67° F.

Chinook Salmon 55° F.

Rainbow Trout 55° F.

Lake Trout 50° F.

Coho Salmon 55° F.

101

WATER TEMPERATURE

In most cases, fish activity is governed by water temperature. It affects their movements and spawning and is an important factor to consider during the various seasons. Most fish prefer a particular water temperature and seek out the depths that suit them best. Learn those depths and you'll catch more fish.

Lure Making

Basic Tools and Materials

The illustrations below and on the next page show some of the basic tools and materials required to make your own lures (including plugs, spinners, jigs, spoons, and buzz baits).

You can purchase most of them at your local tackle shop or through any of the many mail order houses that deal in fishing equipment.

The type of tools and materials you will be using will vary depending on the type of lure you are trying to make.

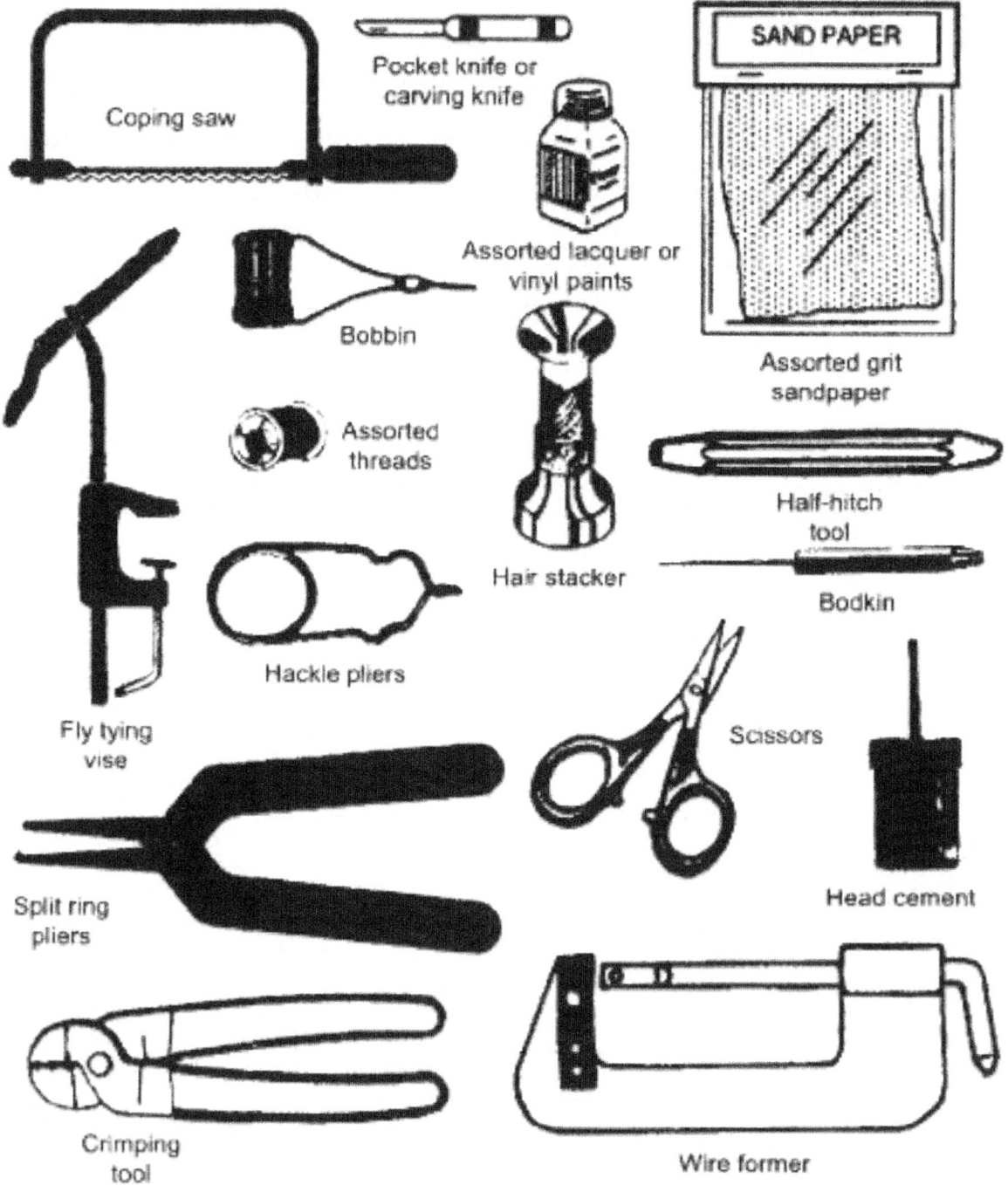

TOOLS

Coping saw

Pocket knife or carving knife

SAND PAPER

Assorted lacquer or vinyl paints

Bobbin

Assorted grit sandpaper

Assorted threads

Hair stacker

Half-hitch tool

Bodkin

Hackle pliers

Fly tying vise

Scissors

Head cement

Split ring pliers

Crimping tool

Wire former

MATERIALS

Assorted feathers

Assorted colored hackles, marabou

Assorted colored yarn, floss, chenille

Assorted tinsel, flashabou, crystal flash

Assorted colored buck tails and calf tails

Assorted colored fur

Assorted spinner blades

Wire in assorted sizes (formed optional)

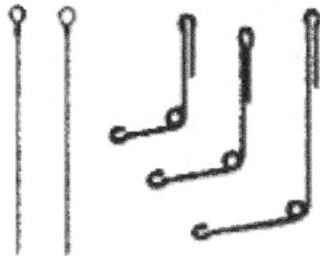

Assorted clevises

Assorted spinner bodies

Spinner shaft locks (springs)

Assorted connector sleeves

Assorted screw eyes

Assorted beads

Assorted barrel swivels

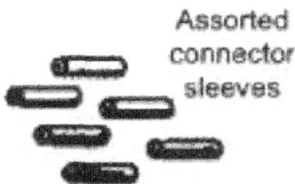

Assorted split rings

Assorted snap swivels

Assorted egg sinkers

Hooks in assorted sizes

Assorted jigs

MATERIALS

The following pages contain the basic instructions for making lures and other types of fishing gear (for example, leaders and slip sinkers). Each type of lure can be varied depending on the materials you use and how creative you want to be.

MAKING PLUGS

You can make a variety of plugs, either from store-bought material (already shaped plastic bodies) or by carving your own from a block of wood.

The following illustrations show the materials, tools, and components required to make your own plugs. Most of the tools can be found in the average home, and the materials or components can be purchased at most tackle shops or from a mail order tackle dealer.

MATERIALS

Selecting the material for the plug you want to build is important.

Most wooden plugs are made of basswood or red cedar. Both of these woods have a smooth grain finish and are easy to carve. You can purchase wood blocks in assorted sizes through most mail order tackle dealers or you can get the wood at your local lumber yard.

REQUIRED TOOLS

Coping saw

Carving knife

SAND PAPER

Sandpaper
(assorted grits)

Plastic cement

Paint
(lacquer or vinyl,
assorted colors)

COMPONENTS

Components such as hooks, plastic-formed bodies, screws, and hook eyes, shown below, must be purchased from your local tackle shop or mail order tackle dealer.

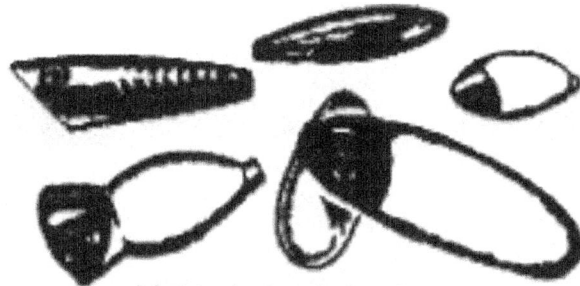

Molded plastic bodies
(assorted shapes)

Treble hooks
(assorted sizes)

Hook eyes
(assorted sizes)

Scoops

Screws
(assorted lengths)

Hook hangers
(assorted sizes)

Cup washers
(assorted sizes)

PLASTIC PLUG ASSEMBLY

STEP 1

Most purchased plastic plug bodies come as two pieces, either a front and a back or a left and right side. Regardless of their type, they must be glued together using plastic plug cement and allowed to dry.

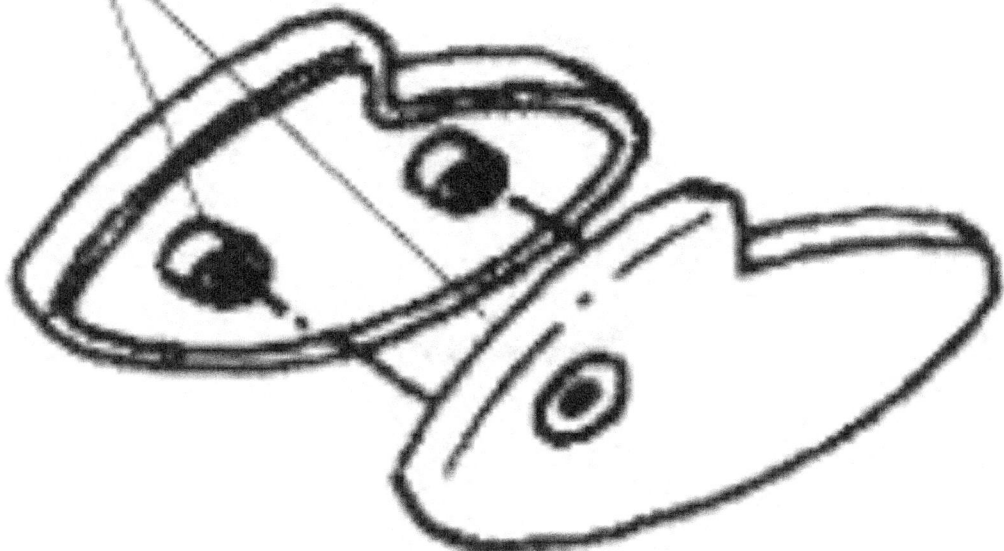

Apply plastic cement to edges

GLUE TOGETHER

STEP 2

After the plug is glued together, remove any burrs or excess cement with a piece of fine grit sandpaper.

Sand smooth

REMOVE BURRS AND SMOOTH

STEP 3

Paint the plug the desired colors using vinyl paints (three coats) and again allow it to dry.

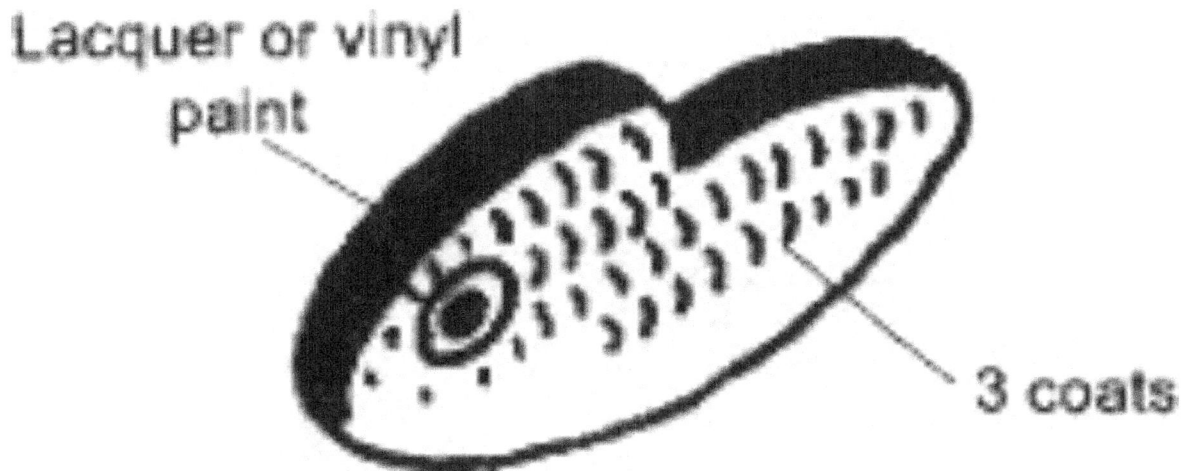

Lacquer or vinyl paint

3 coats

PAINT BODY THREE COATS

STEP 4

After the plug is completely dry, you can attach the hook eyes or hook hangers, hooks, scoop, and line eye to the plug, using a small screwdriver.

Your plug is now complete and ready to use.

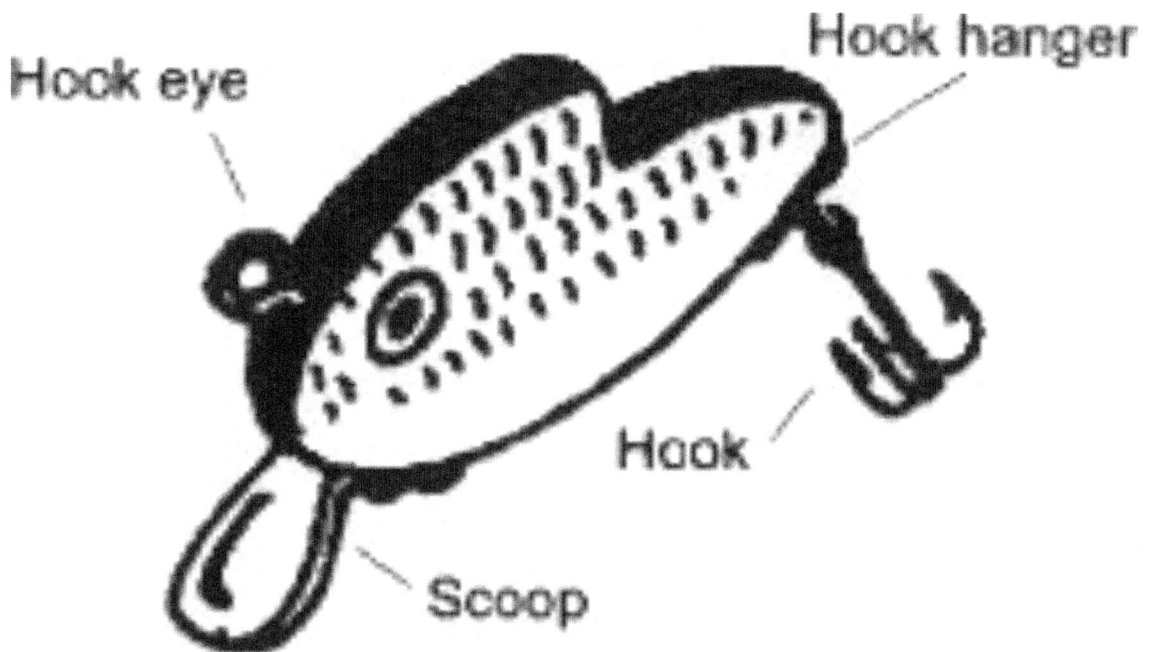

ATTACH HARDWARE

WOODEN PLUGS: CARVING AND ASSEMBLY

The next two pages give examples of the steps necessary to make a wooden plug. The examples shown are for a pan fish plug and a crank bait. The same method used in the construction of both these plugs can be applied to make a wooden equivalent of any of the premolded plugs available today. All it takes is the time and a minimal investment in the tools and components.

PANFISH PLUGS

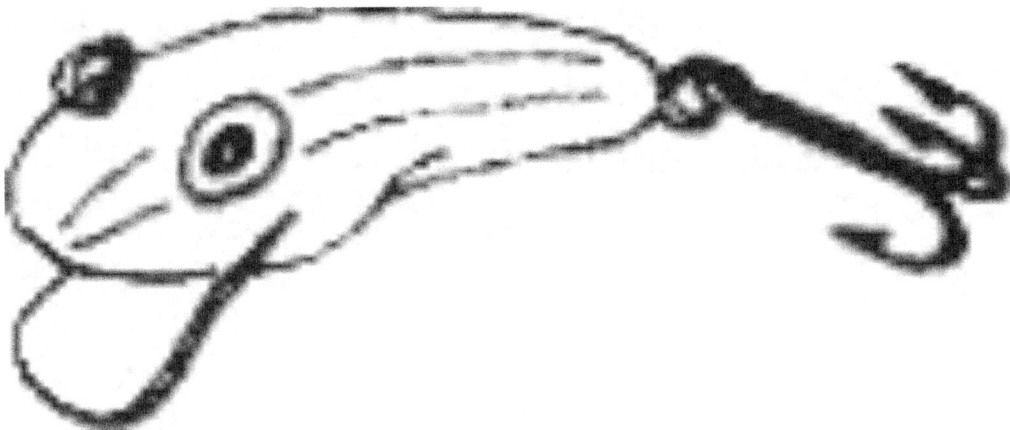

MATERIALS

- One block of basswood or cedar, ¼" thick × ¾" wide × 1-¼" long

- One soda or beer can tab

- Two hook eyes

- One treble hook

- Epoxy cement (glue)

- Light green, black, and white model paint

PATTERN

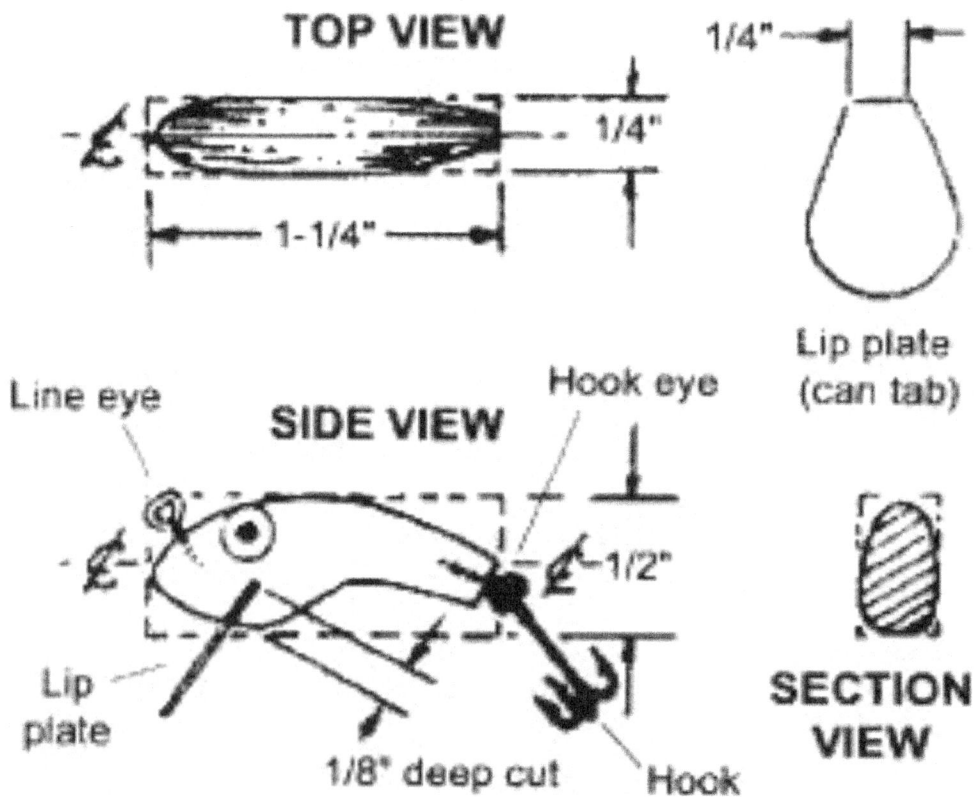

INSTRUCTIONS

STEP 1
Trace the pattern onto the wood block.

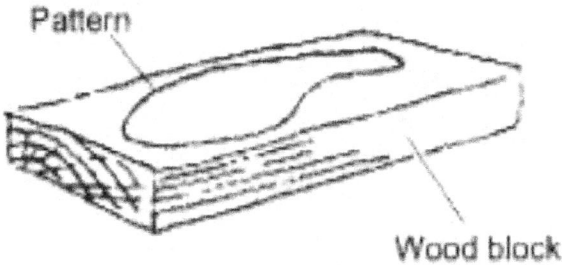

Pattern

Wood block

STEP 2
Cut out the pattern with a coping saw.

Allow pattern
to show

STEP 3
Shape the body with a razor or knife to the proper dimensions and sand smooth with #120 grade sandpaper.

Shape and sand
smooth

STEP 4
Cut a slot for the lip plate with a coping saw per the dimensions below and glue the plate into position.

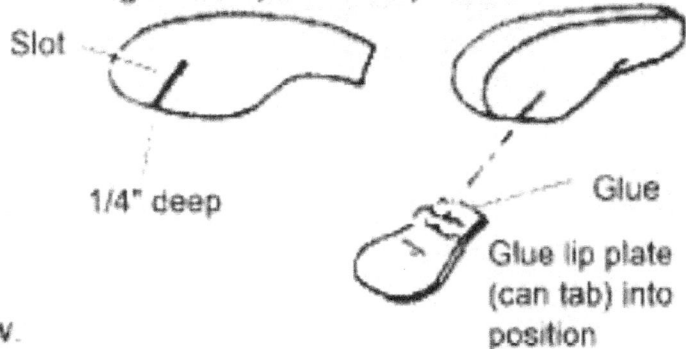

Slot

1/4" deep

Glue

Glue lip plate
(can tab) into
position

STEP 5
Paint the plug body as shown (three coats) and paint in the eyes. After the paint dries, attach the line eye, hook eye, and hook.

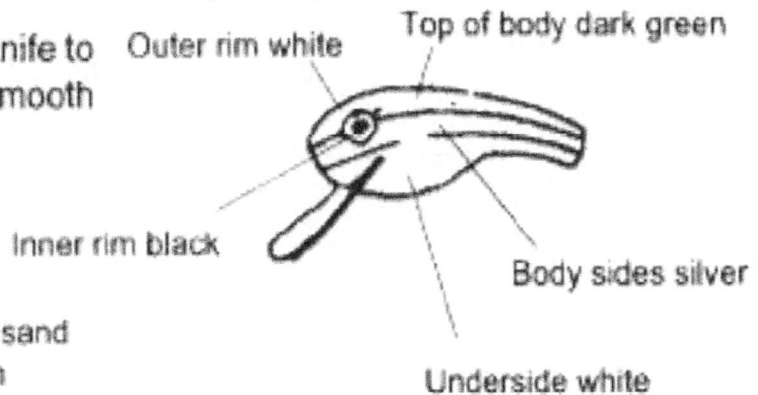

Outer rim white

Top of body dark green

Inner rim black

Body sides silver

Underside white

CRANKBAITS

MATERIALS

- One block of basswood or red cedar, ⅜" thick × ½" wide x 2" long

- One soda or beer can tab

- Two hook eyes

- One treble hook

- Epoxy cement (glue)

- Light green, black, and white model paint

PATTERN

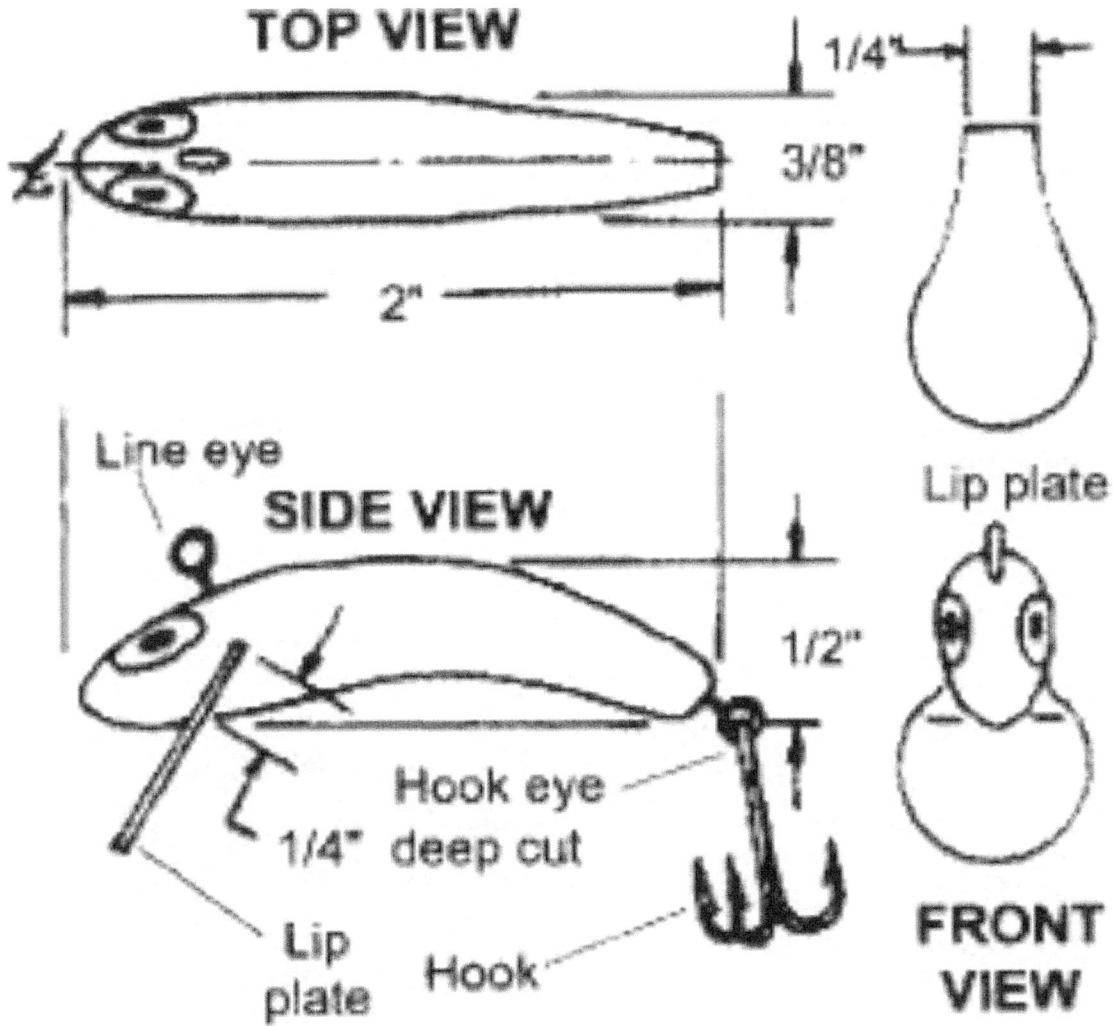

TOP VIEW

1/4"

3/8"

2"

Line eye

SIDE VIEW

Lip plate

1/2"

Hook eye

1/4" deep cut

Lip
plate

Hook

FRONT
VIEW

117

INSTRUCTIONS

STEP 1
Trace the pattern onto the wood block.

Pattern

Slot

Wood block

STEP 2
Cut out the pattern with a coping saw.

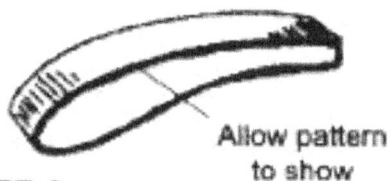

Allow pattern
to show

STEP 3
Shape the body with a razor or knife to the proper dimensions and sand smooth with #120 grade sandpaper.

Shape and sand
smooth

STEP 4
Cut a slot for the lip plate with a coping saw per the dimensions below and glue the plate into position.

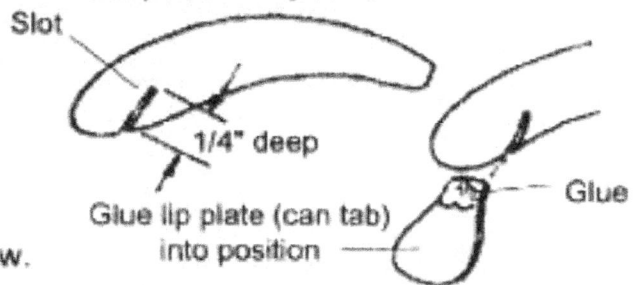

Slot

1/4" deep

Glue lip plate (can tab)
into position

Glue

STEP 5
Paint the plug body as shown (three coats) and paint in the eyes. After the paint dries, attach the line eye, hook eye, and hook.

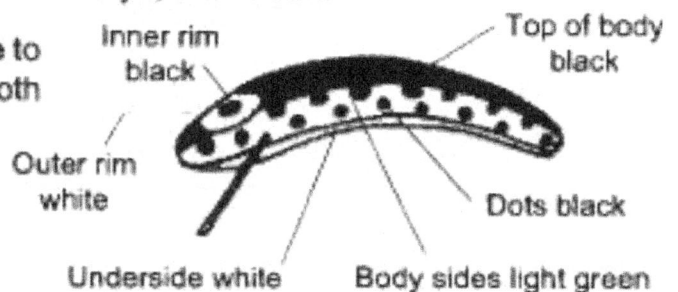

Inner rim
black

Top of body
black

Outer rim
white

Dots black

Underside white

Body sides light green

HOW TO DRESS JIGS

To get started in dressing your own jigs, you will need the following tools and materials.

TOOLS

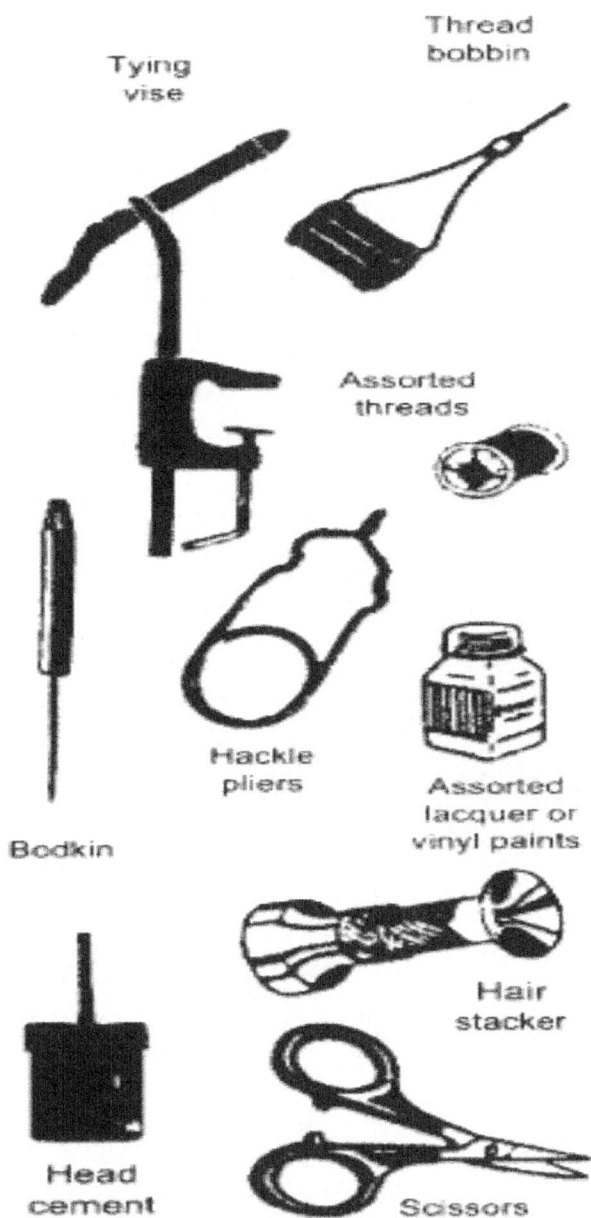

119

MATERIALS

The first requirement in materials for dressing jigs is the jighead itself. You can cast your own if you buy a jig mold, jig hooks, and the lead, or you can purchase pre-cast jigheads at most tackle shops. Many tackle shops carry a vast variety of pre-cast jigs in different sizes, shapes, and colors that are reasonably priced and will eliminate a lot of work involved in casting or painting your own.

The second material requirement is to have an assortment of feathers, furs, and tinsels in a variety of colors. Most of these items can be obtained as individual items or in a jig tying kit, which can also be purchased at most sporting goods stores. The advantage of buying a kit is that it also includes the equipment or tools, such as a vise, bobbin, and hackle pliers, for dressing jigs.

ASSORTED JIGHEADS, FEATHERS, FURS AND TINSELS

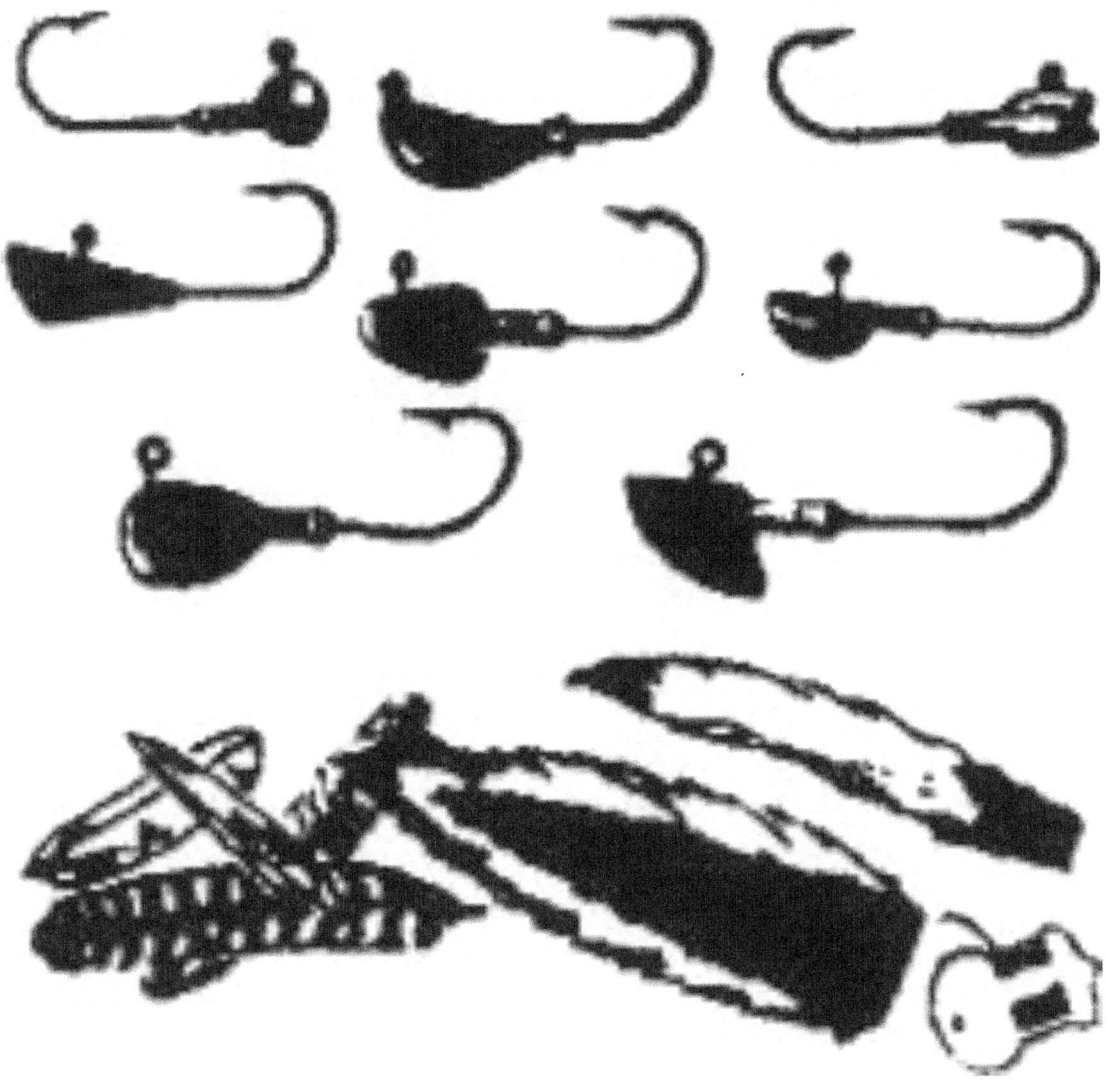

DRESSING

STEP 1

Paint the jighead the desired color and allow it to dry. After it is dry, secure the jighead in the vise as shown below.

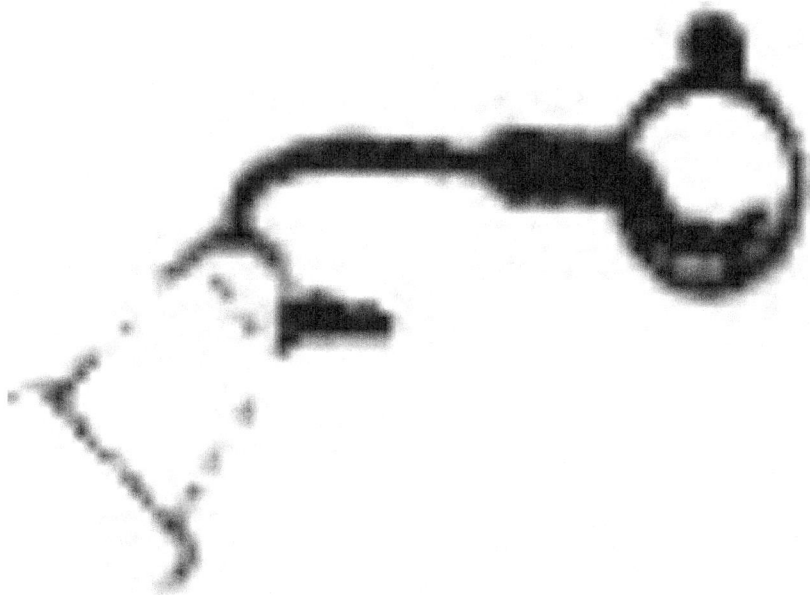

STEP 2

If you are going to have a feather or tinsel tail, lay down a base of thread along the hook shank from the head to the bend of the hook.

STEP 3

Tie in the tail material on top of the thread base and tie off with a half-hitch.

STEP 4

Lay down a thread base along the jighead collar.

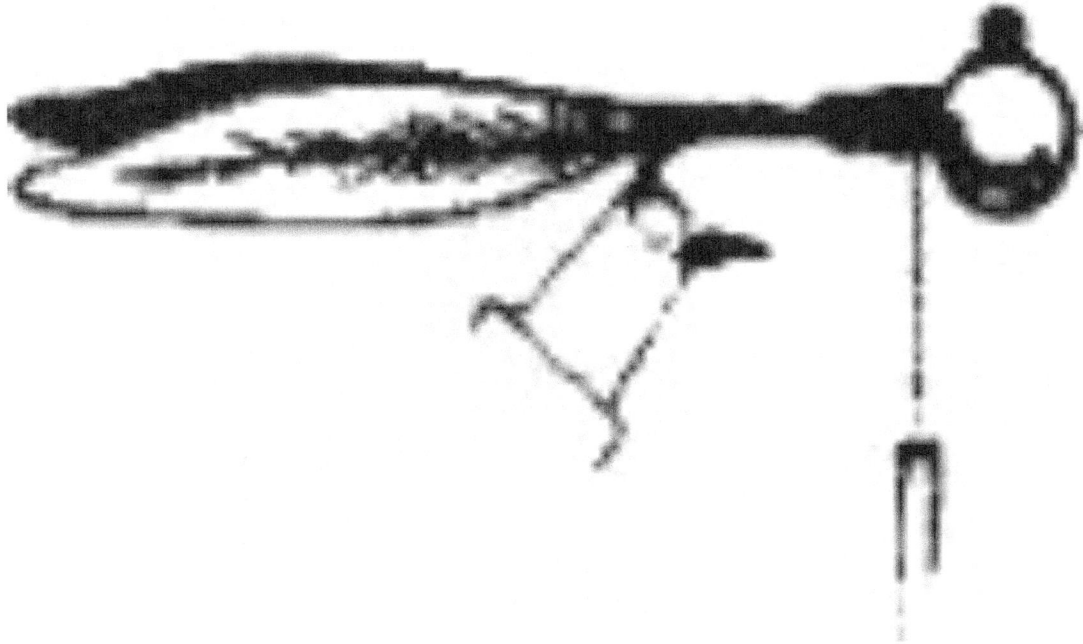

STEP 5

Tie in your choice of material (such as feathers or fur) around the collar, as shown below, and secure it with a half-hitch.

STEP 6

Select a long saddle hackle, strip part of the stem, and tie it in just behind the jighead.

STEP 7

Using your hackle pliers, wrap (palmer) the hackle around the collar (three or four wraps) and secure it with your thread.

STEP 8

Finish off with a couple of half-hitches, tie off (cut the thread), and coat the thread with head cement. Your jig is now complete.

SPOONS

Here's a way to cut down on the costs of buying those expensive ready-made lures. All you need are a few household tools, a few barrel swivels, split rings, and hooks, which can be purchased at a tackle shop for a few pennies, and some old silverware spoons you can pick up at a neighborhood garage sale or flea market.

SILVERWARE SPOONS

STEP 1

Remove the handle from a teaspoon or tablespoon using a hacksaw. Then grind or file the cut end smooth.

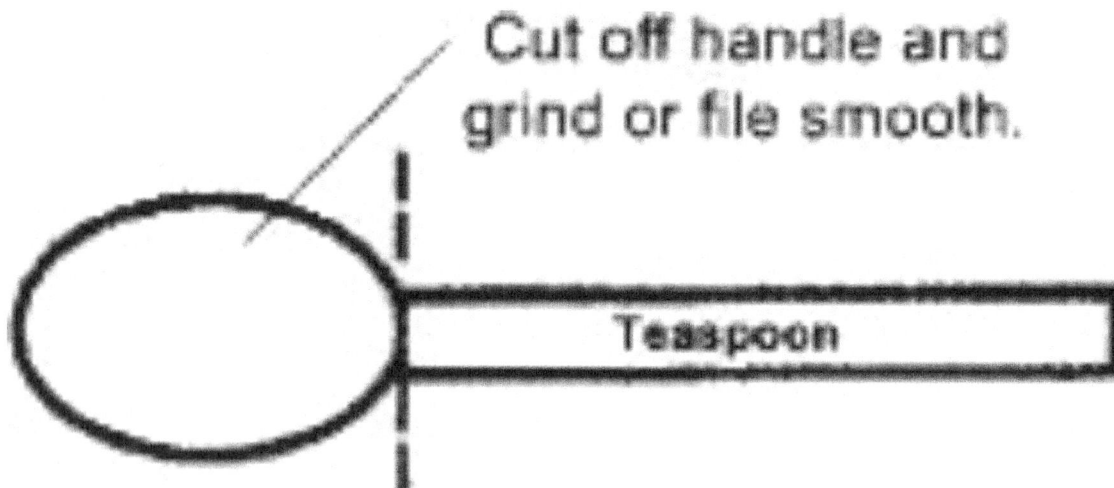

Cut off handle and grind or file smooth.

Teaspoon

STEP 2

Drill a small hole at each end of the spoon as shown below.

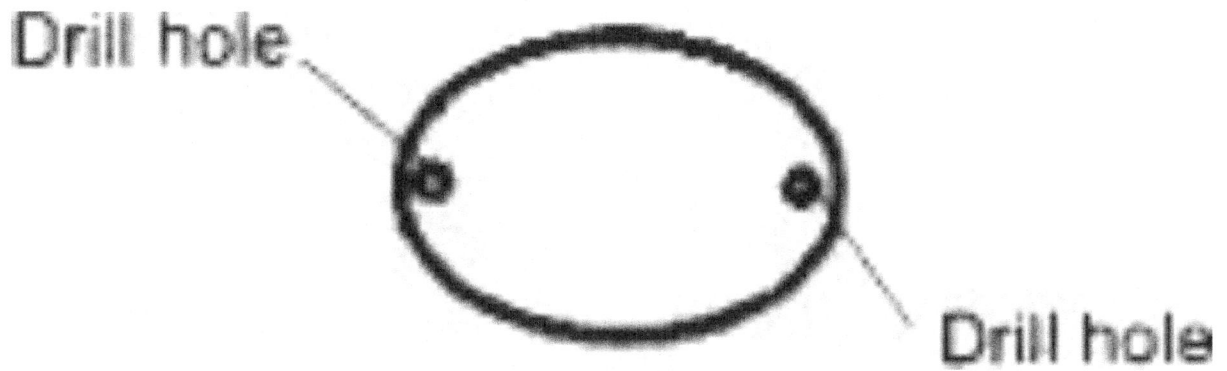

Drill hole

Drill hole

STEP 3

Attach the swivel, split rings, and hook as shown below.

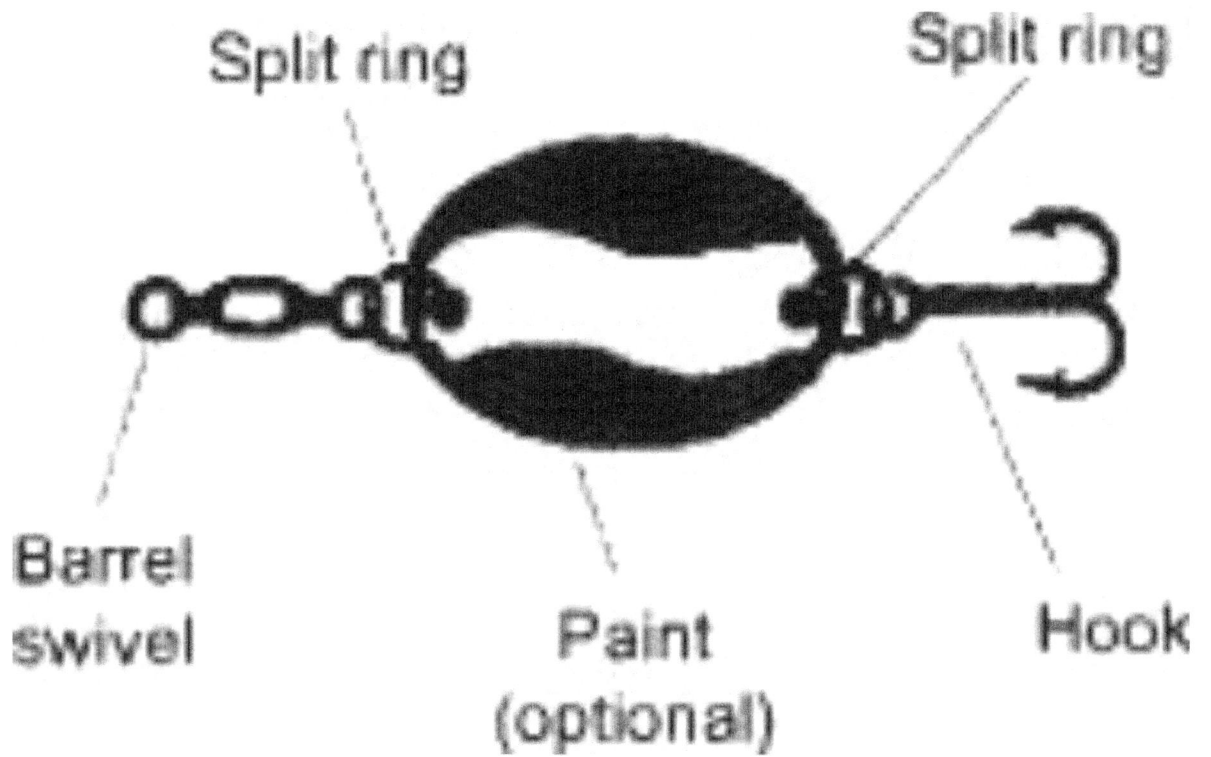

Split ring

Split ring

Barrel
swivel

Paint
(optional)

Hook

SPINNER BLADE SPOONS

Another type of spoon that's easy to make is the spinner blade spoon. All you need are some spinner blades in assorted sizes and styles, which you can purchase at most tackle shops. Then drill another hole at the blade end and attach the swivel, split rings, and hook the same way you did for the silverware spoon.

BLADE STYLES

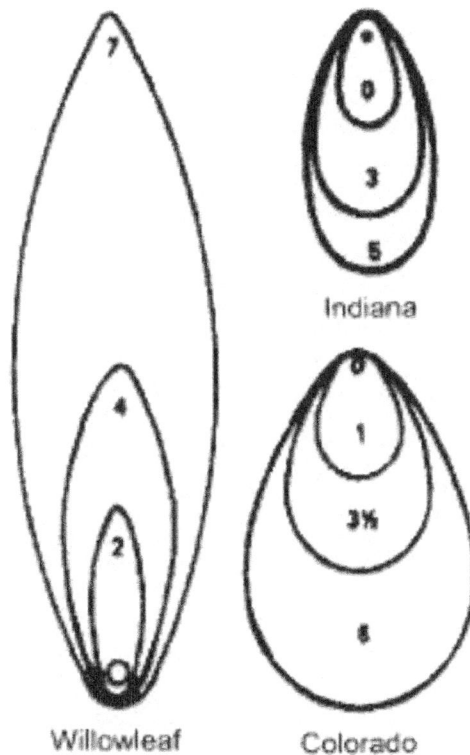

Willowleaf

Indiana

Colorado

For additional flash, put some adhesive-backed prismatic sheet material on the blade.

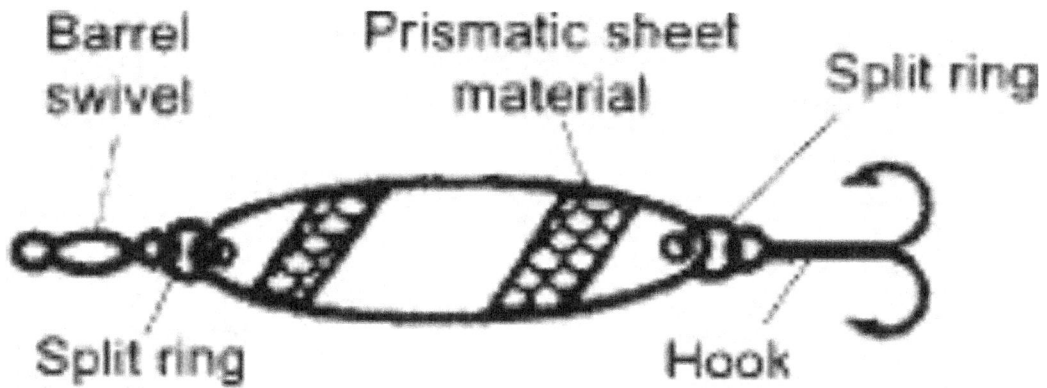

SPOON-MAKING TIP

When making spoons using either silverware or spinner blades, try different-shaped blades or styles.

Each shape has its own action. Some shapes will flutter back and forth and others will wobble.

FLY ROD SPOONS

By using small spinner blades, split rings, and your favorite wet fly or streamer, you can make an effective light spoon for fly casting.

STEP 1

Drill two small holes, one at each end of the spinner blade.

Drill hole

Drill hole

STEP 2

Attach a small split ring through each hole at both ends.

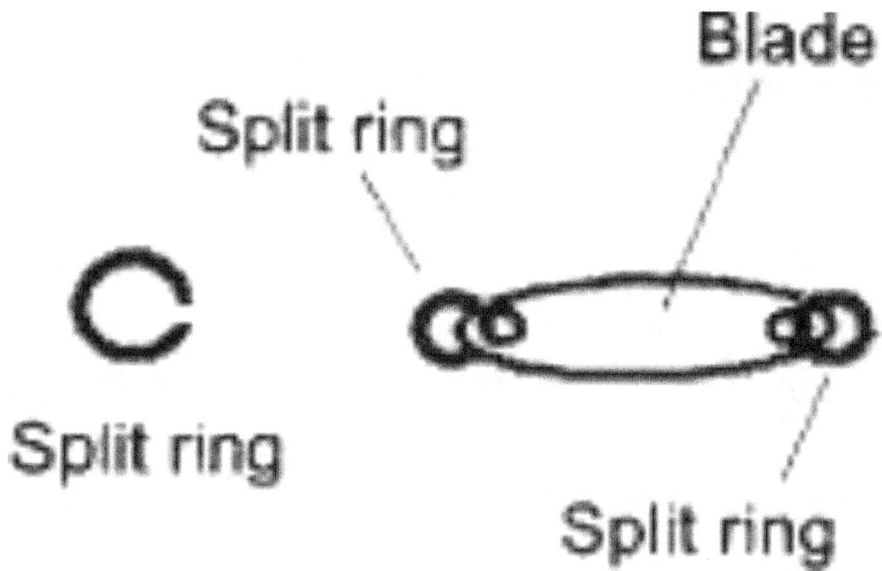

STEP 3

Attach your favorite wet fly or streamer to one of the split rings, as shown below.

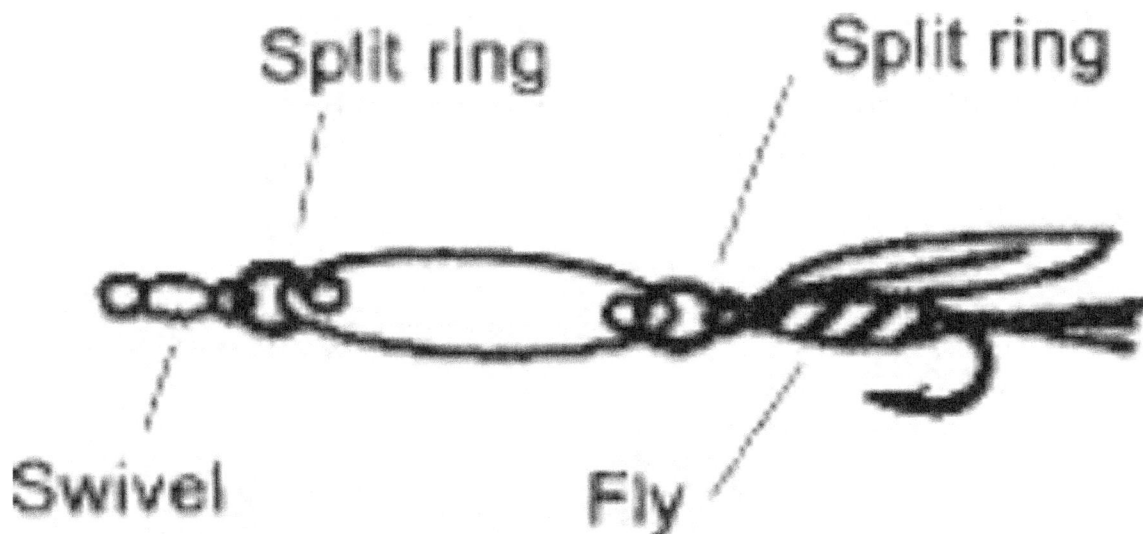

Split ring   Split ring

Swivel   Fly

ICE SPOONS

Here's another type of spoon you can make with a spinner blade. You can use it for ice fishing or fly casting.

STEP 1

Starting with a small spinner blade (sizes 00, 0 or 1), solder a small hook to the inner side of the blade, as shown below.

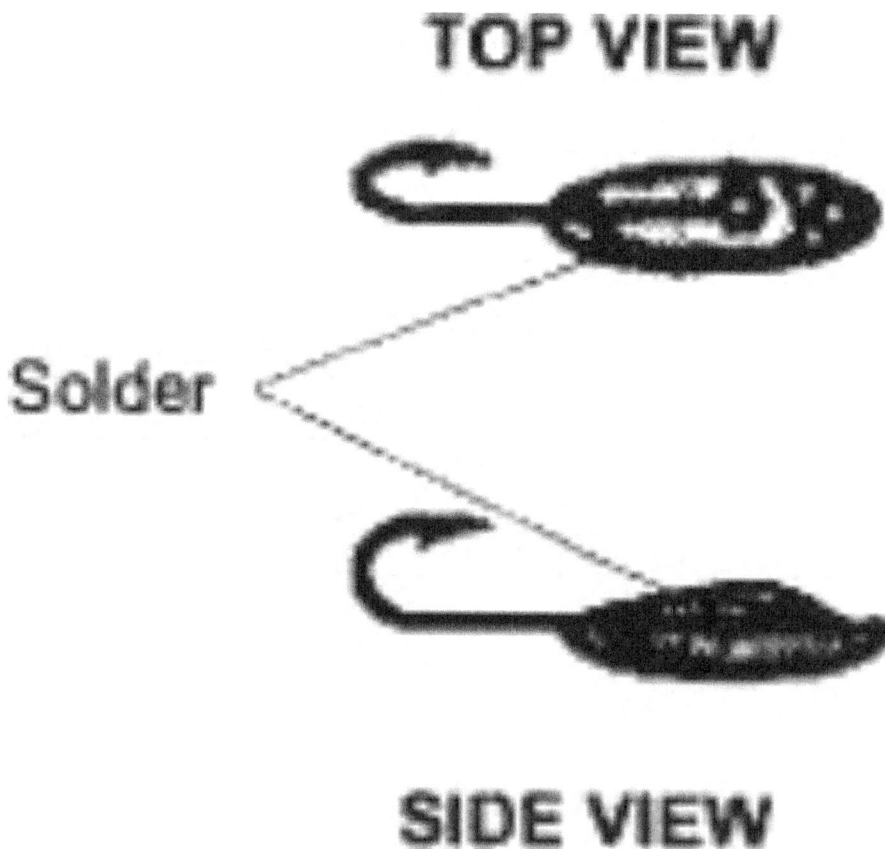

TOP VIEW

Solder

SIDE VIEW

STEP 2

File the soldered surface smooth and paint the entire blade the color of your choice.

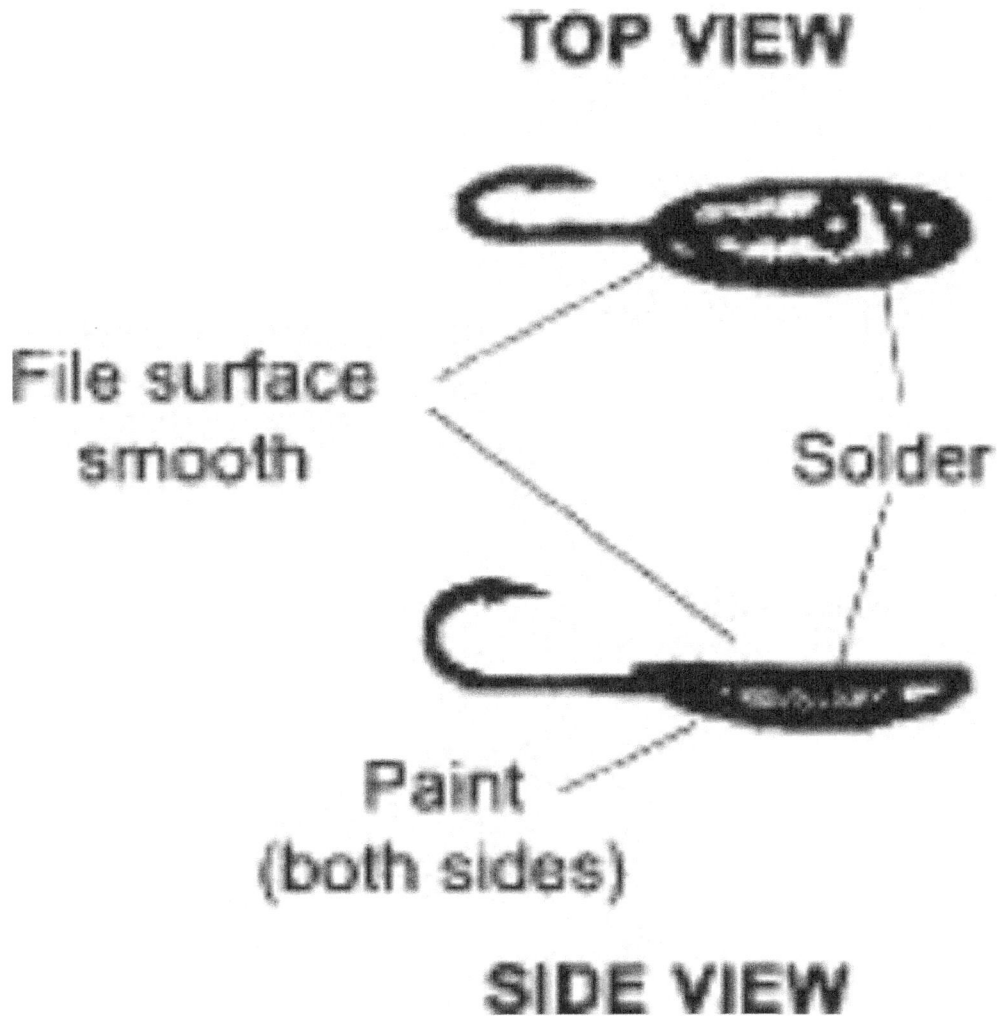

TOP VIEW

File surface smooth

Solder

Paint
(both sides)

SIDE VIEW

SPINNERS

When making a spinner, it is important to remember a few factors as follows.

In most spinner designs, the weight or body should be behind the blade rather than in front of it. If you want the weight or body in front of the blade, it should be fixed to the shaft so it won't slide down and stop the blade from spinning. Keep this in mind when you start your spinner assembly.

To start making spinners, one of the best investments is a wire former. This tool will allow you to form the shafts and all of the bends (eyes, loops, safety pin snap bends) that are required in a spinner construction.

WIRE FORMER TOOL

The wire former shown below is only one of many types available today.

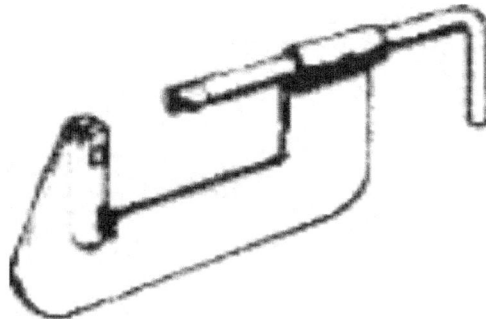

The following illustrations show a few of the many bends that can be made with a wire former.

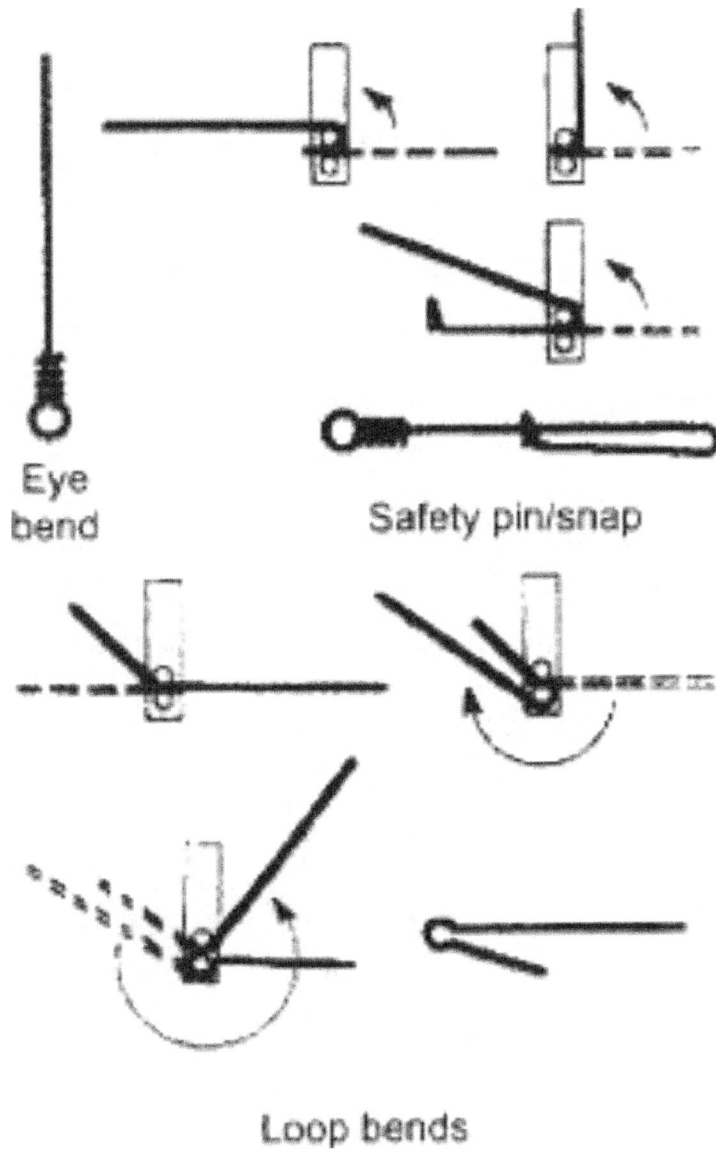

Eye
bend

Safety pin/snap

Loop bends

NAIL METHOD FOR BENDS AND LOOPS

If you don't have a wire forming tool, here's an alternative way to make the bends and loops on purchased shafts that have a wrapped eye, which will require additional bending.

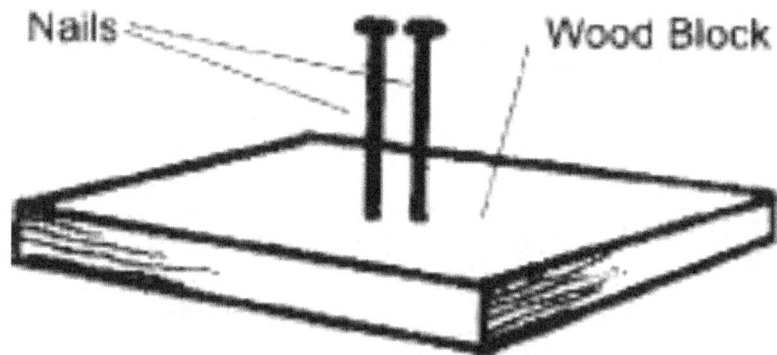

Just pound a couple of nails into a wooden block far enough apart to slip the wire between them. Make the bends as shown below.

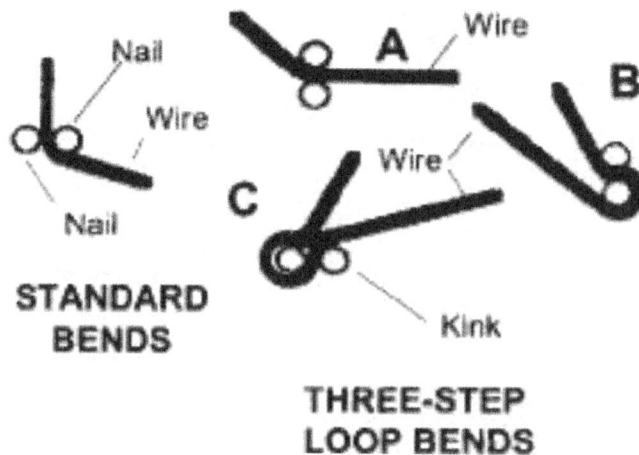

STANDARD BENDS

THREE-STEP LOOP BENDS

SPINNER COMPONENTS AND ASSEMBLY

To make your own spinners you will need certain components, which are illustrated below.

With the exception of the wire shafts, which can be formed with a wire former, you can purchase the majority of the components from your local tackle shop or through a mail order tackle supply catalog at a reasonable price.

COMPONENTS

Wire shafts
wrapped eye
closed loop
(assorted gages)

Coil springs

Beads
glass or brass
(assorted colors)

Treble hooks
(assorted sizes)

Clevis
(assorted sizes)

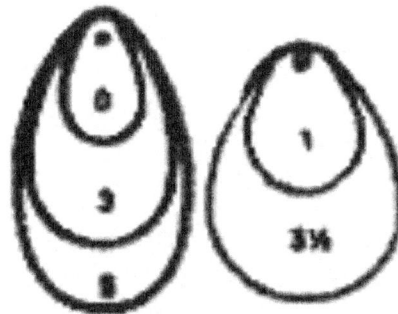

Spinner blades
(assorted
styles and sizes)

Brass bodies
(assorted)

ASSEMBLY

STEP 1

Starting with the wire shaft, slip on the components in the following order.

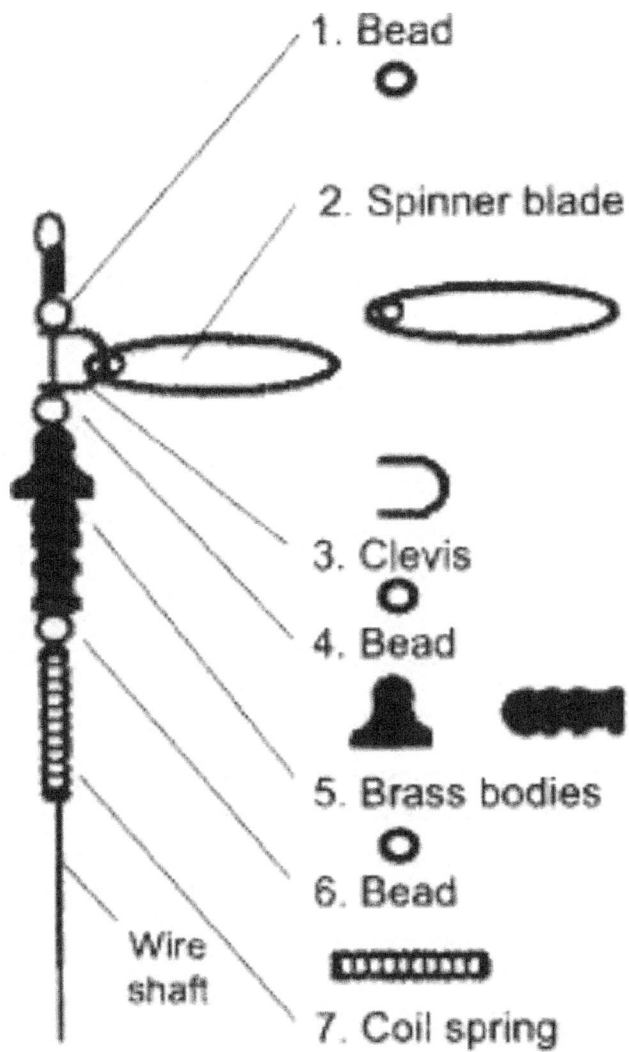

1. Bead

2. Spinner blade

3. Clevis

4. Bead

5. Brass bodies

6. Bead

Wire shaft

7. Coil spring

STEP 2

After all the components are on the shaft, make an open loop bend on the unbent part of the shaft using the wire former or a pair of pliers, as shown below.

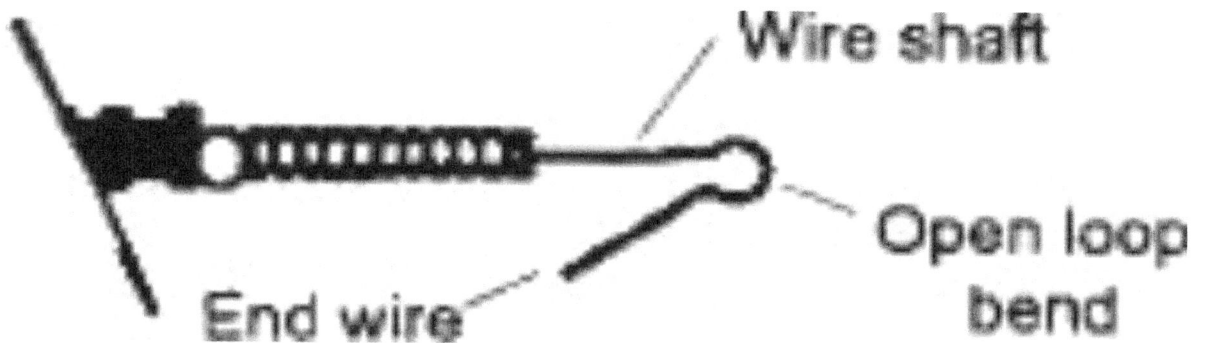

Wire shaft

Open loop bend

End wire

STEP 3

After the bend is made, trim the end wire so that the coil spring can be pulled down, as shown below.

Coil spring over wire

Add hook

BUZZBAITS

Buzzbaits are a common lure used for fishing bass as well as other species. The lure is fished by using a fast retrieve, causing the blade to churn the water surface, which creates a commotion that attracts fish.

The items shown below are the tools and components required to make a buzzbait. You can make the body of the lure by using a wire former and attaching a jig, as shown in the instructions, or you can use purchased preformed bodies for the assembly. You can also cast your own body forms with the jig in place by using a buzzbait mold.

The pre-formed bodies or the buzzbait mold, as well as the delta blades shown below, can be purchased from most tackle shops or mail order tackle supply houses.

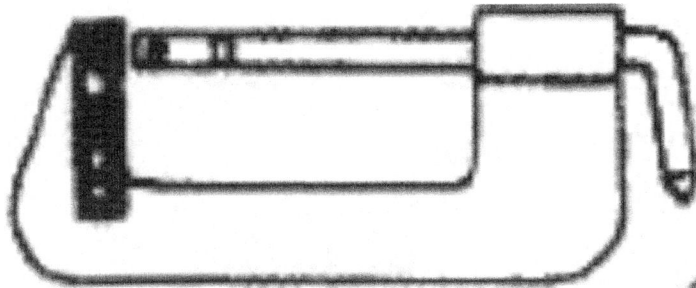

Wire
former

Jig paint
(assorted colors)

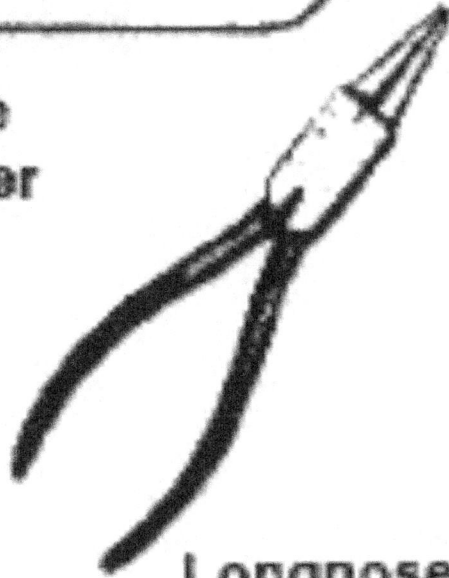

Longnose
pliers

Crimping
tool

TOOLS

MOLDING TOOLS (OPTIONAL)

Buzzbait mold

Casting ladle

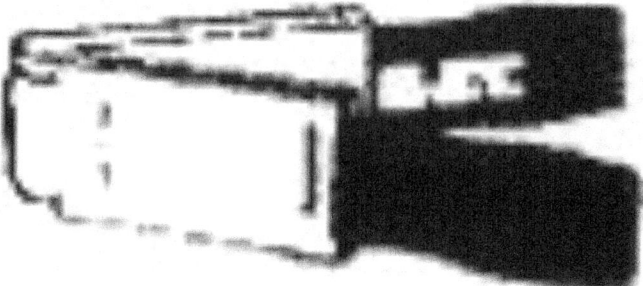

Casting lead

COMPONENTS

Wire
(assorted gages)

Buzzbait body forms
pre-cast (optional)

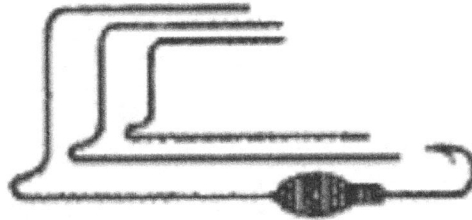

Pre-cast jigs
(assorted)

Delta blades
(assorted sizes)

Blade collars
rivets
(assorted sizes)

Brass or glass beads
(assorted colors
and sizes)

Connector sleeves
(assorted sizes)

Rubber skirts
(assorted colors)

151

WIRE BODY CONSTRUCTION

The following instructions for forming the basic wire for a buzzbait apply only if you choose to make your own form.

Starting with a 12-inch piece of wire (.028 or .035 diameter), form the wire to the proportions shown at right.

Note: *The larger or heavier the jighead, the larger diameter wire.*

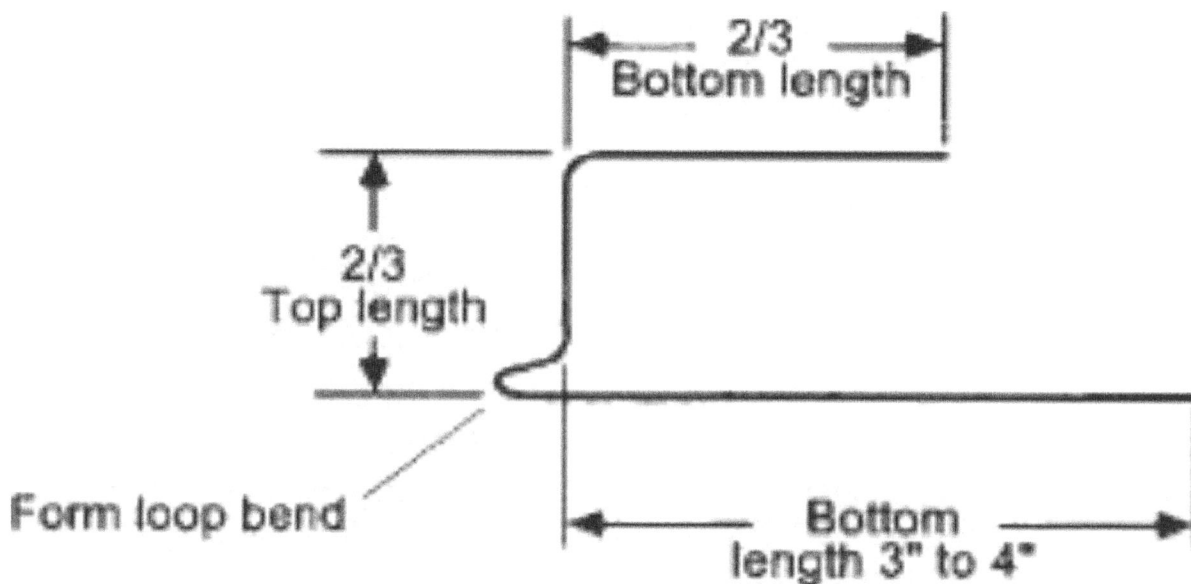

ASSEMBLY

STEP 1

Begin by painting the jighead, whether it is a pre-formed casted wire with the head attached or a loose jighead. Next, slip the blade collar (narrow end first) or a bead onto the top wire, as shown in the illustration below.

STEP 2

Slip the delta blade or tandem blades onto the top wire, as shown below, followed by several beads. After the components are in place, bend the end of the wire slightly with your longnose pliers. With the pre-formed casted wire, your buzzbait is now complete. If you formed your own wire, go to the next step.

STEP 3

Slip a connector sleeve (proper diameter for wire gage being used) onto the bottom wire, followed by the loose jighead, and form a loop bend in the bottom wire approximately where the top wire ends. Move the jighead back to the loop and slip the open end of the bottom wire into the connector sleeve, crimping the sleeve with your crimping tool. Finish off your buzzbait by slipping on a rubber skirt.

How to Pick and Purchase Tackle for Fishing with Kids

Fishing is a wonderful pastime that can be enjoyed alone, with a friend, or with the family. Taking your children fishing is a great way to nurture the parent and child bond, as well as develop a mutual love for the sport of fishing and the great outdoors. Fishing with the kids does require a little extra preparation and planning, but you'll be happy you made the effort in the end. Aside from safety precautions, there are a few other things you need to think about such as how to pick and purchase tackle for fishing with kids.

* Keep It to Scale

Trying to teach a child to fish with a regular adult sized pole is probably not the best idea. Adult sizes are too large for the child to handle properly, so try to keep everything scaled down to their size so that they can learn to handle the rod, reel, and tackle box items correctly. By the time they reach the point where they can handle an adult sized rod and reel, they'll be old pros.

* Children's Rods and Reels

Many companies today make child sized rod and reel combination sets that are not only smaller sized, but also come in popular character themes that both boys and girls will love. Set your daughter up with an adorable Barbie or Disney Princess rod and reel set, or set your son up with a cool Spiderman, Star Wars, or Cars rod and reel combination. Combination rod and reel sets also come in a Mickey Mouse theme, suitable for either a boy or a girl. To make it even just a little bit cooler, the Mickey Mouse pole comes with a light on it that is sure to impress your little one. These little rods are only two and a half feet long, the perfect size for little hands to hold onto and control.

* Children's Tackle Boxes

Giving a child their own child sized tackle box will make them feel proud. They can carry around their own little box that is designed to be just right for small hands to hold and open and close. Some of the fishing rod and reel sets mentioned above are offered in "fishing bundles" that include both the rod and reel combo as well as the tackle box. Tackle boxes coordinate with the rod and reel set, including designs such as Barbie, Spiderman, Cars, and others. Kids will appreciate the fact that they have their own tackle box, just like dad or mom. The bundle packages are reasonably priced too, selling for around $20 to $26 at many retailers.

If you're interested in a tackle box for beginners that already comes with the included tackle, the South Bend Worm Gear Tackle Box makes a great choice. The box comes loaded with eighty eight pieces of fishing gear, including an assortment of hooks, multi-colored bobbers, brass swivels, lead free split shot, hook disgorger, and more. This set is ideal for beginners because of the ease of replacing hooks and lures that this kit offers.

* Choosing the Right Tackle

When choosing tackle, remember to keep things small. Chances are your child will be using worms as bait, so choose small ones such as wax worms. They are fairly easy to handle and just the right size for catching small fish such as bluegill. Use smaller hooks that you would for an adult, and if choosing to use a lure, pick small ones instead of the sizes that are probably close to that of the fish which they will actually end up catching.

* Children's Backpack Fishing Kit

When purchasing tackle and fishing equipment for kids, there are also convenient backpacks available that include a small, foldable rod and reel set that fits conveniently in the pack, small fishing kit, and practice casting plug. Another important thing to mention about these backpack kits is that the included items meet CPSC safety requirements. Kit also includes a handy pair of child's sunglasses. These backpacks can be purchased in Barbie, Disney Princess, Cars, and Star Wars themes to delight the kids.

Conclusion

Taking the kids fishing may require a little extra effort and planning, but the memories will be treasured for a lifetime. Make sure to invest in a proper fitting child's life jacket before your trip. With a little planning, and by choosing gear that fits the child, you'll be all set for a wonderful experience that both you and the kids will remember for years to come

Safety Tips for kid fishing

A family day spent on the water is a great way to have some wholesome fun together. There are a couple of safety tips that you need to keep in mind while fishing with kids. The joy of watching a child catch their first fish can be overshadowed by injury. So, as an adult, you need to ensure your child's safety before you do anything else. In this section, you will learn about the different safety tips you need to follow while fishing with kids.

Protective Eyewear

The first safety tip for fishing safely with kids is to use protective eyewear. To reduce strain on the eyes while spotting fish, use polarized sunglasses. Not just that, it will also offer protection from branches and lures while fishing. If you want to go fishing at night, you must also include a pair of clear glasses. You can buy clear glasses from a local hardware store.

Barbless Hooks

Always use barbless hooks because. They are easier to remove if a child or adult is snagged. These hooks are quite important when you are bait fishing and when you are using them, you need to slightly bend them down.

PFD's

PFD refers to a personal floatation device. Anyone can accidentally fall into the water, and to avoid accidents, always include a PFD in your fishing kit. A PFD is a must if you put the kids in a kayak, canoe, or a boat while fishing.

Set Ground Rules

You need to set some clearly defined rules and you need to make sure that the children follow these rules. Kids certainly love to have fun, but it is a recipe for disaster if they start running around a wet boat deck. You need to teach the child certain fishing skills as well as etiquette. You need to set some rules ahead of time and ensure that the children abide by them. This is incredibly important if you are fishing with a toddler. You are responsible for their safety and you need to teach the children about being safe while having fun. Also, setting certain rules reduces the risk of any accidents.

Nourishment

Never forget to carry drinks and snacks with you while going fishing. You will need sufficient snacks and water to prevent dehydration. Also, you never know when the child might be hungry! So, having a couple of snacks on hand is a good idea.

Kid-friendly Tackle

There are some rods that can be quite heavy, and a young child cannot handle these fishing rods well. The fishing equipment you use must be child-friendly. So, spend some time going through the list of ideal fishing gear and equipment given in this book.

Fishing Gear

Safety for kids while fishing also includes appropriate clothing. You always need to keep the kids warm and dry. So, you will need rain jackets or windcheaters, woolens to stay warm and a pair of boat shoes or sneakers to help with easy movement.

First-aid Kit

You need a first aid kit and; never do outdoor activities without carrying one with you. A typical first aid kit needs to include band-aids, bandages, gauze, disinfectant, pain medication, cotton, and allergy medication.

Whistle

Yeah, carrying a whistle might make you look like a coach or a lifeguard, but whenever the kids start to stray, a blast or two will certainly get them back.

If you keep all these things in mind, you will be able to handle almost any situation that comes your way and you can focus on fishing.

How to Have Fun Even if the Fish Aren't Biting

Most adults in the United States have gone fishing at least once in their lives as children. Sometimes they caught fish and sometimes they did not. As they grew older, the memories of the trips where they did not catch anything will fade. They will always remember, though, that first fish you caught as a child.

When it comes time to take your child fishing, most people are concerned that they the child will not have fun. The question, how can a fishing trip be fun when you're not catching fish, often comes up.

There are plenty of ways to ensure your child has fun and learns to love fishing. Catching fish is part of it but so is the experience, the parent-child bonding and the lessons that you can learn.

Getting Started

Get your child involved in the preparations. Young children love to help mom or dad though the older ones may try to avoid doing so! Make the preparation time something that you and your son or daughter do together. Get out your gear, go to the bait shop together, and pack the car with drinks and snacks or lunch. Make it an adventure that just you and your child are sharing.

Take the time to show your boy or girl the equipment you will be using before you go. Show them how a rod works, the line, baiting the hook and the bobs and sinkers.

Remember to talk about safety. You like will not let a young child bait a hook on their trip, but you can let them watch you do it, ask questions and throw the line in by themselves.

Water safety is also important. Put on your child's safety jacket and make sure they understand that, assuming you are going to be on a boat, that he or she need to be wearing one at all times. Set the example too and make sure you wear a life jacket also.

Make the first experience easy by ensuring your child has a simple rod and reel. A plastic child's rod is probably best. That way they can have something of their own that relates to their fishing experience.

Location

While one of the lessons of fishing is patience, it is impractical to expect a young child to be able to stay out on a boat for seven hours waiting for a fish to nibble on his or her line.

For this reason, it is probably best to start your child off fishing by doing so from a bank rather than going out in a boat. The best place to start is a small lake or pond where you know that the fish are biting. There are places that have stocked ponds that can give you pretty good odds that your child will be able to catch something.

Other Points to Consider

Remember you are with a child. Do not stay out too long. Going for one or two hours is about all a small child can handle.

Make sure that during the trip you focus on the child's fishing and not your own. Don't expect to try out that new rod and reel or some new spot that may or may not have fish biting.

Wherever you decide to go, be sure that you fish for appropriately sized fish. Go to a location where there are lots of small fish that your child can easily reel in by his or herself. They may get scared or put off by a large, thrashing fish that pulls them into the water or is too heavy for them to maintain a grip on the rod.

How to Fight Boredom

Limiting your time when you go fishing for the first time will help fight boredom somewhat, but children get bored very quickly. If the fish are not biting, they probably will not be able to sit still.

Let them take plenty of breaks. Choose a place near a woods or camping area. Let them explore, maybe look for turtles for a while, or go hunting butterflies.

Make sure you have a cooler with plenty of drinks and snacks. Make the eating a picnicking ritual. Maybe bring a table cloth, plastic cups, tableware and make setting up the picnic spot their responsibility.

You can also build a fire and let them roast marshmallows on a stick. Take them for a hike to break up the day, and then go back to fishing later.

Fishing does not have to be boring. It can be fun and exciting even if your child does not catch anything the first time. You can be assured though that when your child catches that first fish, he or she will be sure to want to go again.

Conclusion

Rules of fishing might seem quite complicated to adults, let along children. You must never bombard children with a whole bunch of rules. Instead, explain in simple terms about things like licenses, size and gear restrictions. You need to teach children that poaching is frowned upon and that it is an illegal activity. Please tell that they can get into trouble if they don't follow fishing regulations, they can get into trouble.

Educate them about the fishing rules and tell them that those rules are in place to ensure that there is sufficient fish for everyone to catch. If a child wants to hold onto his or her catch, that's perfectly all right. If your child wants to eat his or her catch, then that is the right time to explain that you must only retain the catch that you want to eat and release the rest into the wild.

Fishing is an excellent means to teach children to appreciate and respect nature. You can teach your child about the different parts of the fish anatomy while fishing. Water bodies are also home to several other creatures like minnows, macroinvertebrates and crawdads.

You must teach the child that fishing needs to be done sensibly and responsibly. Your acts must not disrupt the delicate balance of the ecosystem that we are a part of. Whenever you go fishing and manage to catch a protected species, you need to make sure that you immediately release it into the wild. You need to protect and respect nature

Fishing is an activity that will provide you with memories and a perfect activity for bonding with children. Another remarkable aspect of fishing is that you have an opportunity to teach the kids about nature and how they need to respect it. Regardless of what you do, you must not force any activity on the child. If the kid asks you that he or she wants to leave, then it is time to head home. Don't exceed an hour or so on the first fishing trip. Once the child is big enough, you both will have an everyday activity to bond over.

Now, all that you need to do is take the first step and take your child on a fishing trip! Remember, safety first when it comes to any outdoor activity that involves your children. Thank you for your time and attention, and I wish you good luck fishing with your little one.

Made in the USA
Monee, IL
29 November 2022

19015251R00092